John Gorman

GORY TALES

John Gorman

THE AUTOBIOGRAPHY
With Kevin Brennan

GORY TALES

Foreword by Glenn Hoddle

Green**Umbrella**
Publishing

This edition first published in the UK in 2008
By Green Umbrella Publishing

© Green Umbrella Publishing 2008

www.gupublishing.co.uk

Publishers: Jules Gammond and Vanessa Gardner

Creative Director: Kevin Gardner

Picture Credits: Getty Images and John Gorman

Printed and bound by J. H. Haynes & Co. Ltd., Sparkford

ISBN: 978-1-906229-86-3

DEDICATION

I suppose you could say I am a typical football nut. I've been mad about the game ever since I was a kid growing up in Scotland. I'm lucky enough to have earned a very decent living from the sport as a player, manager and coach. In many ways football has been my life. But early in 2006 two things happened just weeks apart that made me realise there is so much more to life than football.

The first was the death of a promising young player I managed. The second was even more personal, when my darling wife Myra lost her battle to beat the cancer that had invaded her body, and I held her hand as she slipped peacefully away in her special lounge at home.

Don't get me wrong, I still love the game and enjoy being involved in it to this day, but if I said I view it in quite the same way as I once did, I'd be lying. Football is wonderful and I will never lose my enthusiasm for it or the will to win matches. But I do believe I have a perspective now that didn't quite exist for me once upon a time.

When you see a young kid's life snuffed out because of a car accident, and witness at close quarters the suffering endured by the woman you've loved all of your adult life, it would be pretty amazing if it didn't affect the way you think. Not just about football, but about life, and I hope my story reflects that.

Myra's death has probably been the biggest thing I have had to deal with in my life, and the shock waves of her passing away only really started to hit me weeks after she had gone. There is not a day that goes by without me thinking of her and I know that will be the case for the rest of my life. She was such a wonderful person and I thank God that I was lucky enough to have been married to her. There's no doubt in my mind that I wouldn't have done half the things I have without her love and support. Let's face it, any woman who can endure 22 house moves during her husband's career and still laugh about it, has to be a bit special!

She was there right at the start of my journey and through all the good and bad times. Without her love and support I can't imagine what I would have done and one of the biggest motivating factors in writing this book was the opportunity to put down in words just what she meant to me and the part she played in my story.

I am a football man and have been all my working life. I've been fortunate to have had a career which has spanned five decades, and have seen massive changes take place during that time. Not all of them have been for the good, but there is now no doubt that the sport today operates on a completely different level, both in the way it is played and also financially, to when I first started out with Celtic during their golden European Cup winning era of the 1960's.

It's a very long time to have been involved in the game and I wouldn't have missed a minute of it. Football and my family have always been the two most important things for me. Sometimes I didn't always get the balance right, and like lots of football folk I devoted too much time to a game that can become all-consuming.

Having worked at the very highest level with England's national team as well as with players in non-league, I can tell you there is one common thread that unites all of us involved in what is often a crazy business. It's an addiction to the sport.

Myra together with our two kids Amanda and Nick always seemed to understand this and made my life so much easier as a consequence.

This book is dedicated to them.

CONTENTS

John Gorman

FOREWORD

I can distinctly remember the first time I met John. It was a misty morning at the Tottenham training ground in Cheshunt and I was just getting out of my car when he came through the gates with the Spurs manager Keith Burkinshaw. When I shook hands with John that day I would never have thought that more than 30 years later we would still be working together, and I also had no way of knowing that he would become one of the best friends I could ever have.

It has been a friendship that neither of us could have envisaged back then in 1976, for a start I was just 19 at the time and John was eight years older, and in many ways our personalities were quite opposite, but for some reason we just clicked.

The more we got to know each other the more we seemed to get on, and when it came to football we both had the same thoughts about the way the game should be played. I also liked John as a player. He was a left-back but loved to get forward and had the ability to attack people and pass the ball well. It was easy playing in the same team as him and off the field I quickly got to know John and his lovely wife Myra. I even used to baby-sit their children, Nick and Amanda, for them on occasions because we lived quite close to each other.

It was a terrible shame that John's injury problems at Tottenham limited his appearances for the club, but his determination to continue his career saw him move to the States and play some great football over there. America was good for John, and John was good for America. He's a very open, honest and emotional person. Americans loved him and rightly so.

GORY TALES

When the time came for me to take my first steps in management at Swindon John was always going to be my first choice as an assistant. It wasn't just about friendship, it was also about the fact that I knew we would be singing from the same sheet when it came to the way we were going to try and get the team to play.

I think we both had some of the happiest times of our careers at Swindon, including getting them into the Premiership. Leaving to take over at Chelsea wasn't easy for me and I knew that John felt the same way, even though he'd agreed to join me at Stamford Bridge. When he decided at the very last moment to stay and become Swindon's manager it was a bit of a shock for me, but it didn't take long for us to get over the incident and we were very quickly talking to each other about our new jobs. Those are the sort of things you can overcome when you've got the deep friendship we have.

I know a few eyebrows may have been raised when I asked John to be my assistant when I became England manager, but once again he was always going to be my first choice. As England manager one of the things you look for is trust, and I knew I had that with John. We were on the same wavelength and I knew I could delegate without having to worry about anything he would do. I also realised what a good coach he was, especially when it came to working with players in a one-to-one situation. We've also always had a laugh together and having a good sense of humour can be so important when you're working so closely with someone.

After England John and I worked together at Southampton and at Tottenham. I'm happy that we have got the chance to work together once more, with John joining me as one of my coaches at the football academy I have set up, aiming to offer a route back into the professional game for some of the young players who are discarded by the system.

John Gorman

John seems to relish the prospect of working with these players and helping to improve their game. I recently had to virtually drag him off the training pitch because he just wanted to carry on coaching, but it was great to see that old enthusiasm back.

He is a naturally bubbly, happy and compassionate person. So too was his wife Myra. She was an absolutely lovely lady and I instantly took to her. Our families had some wonderful times together over the years. John and Myra were a great couple and she was always so supportive when it came to his career. She would go anywhere that football took him, never once complaining and sacrificed an awful lot for him.

When she died I was in shock and I have to admit that I couldn't get my head around the situation for some time. I know a lot of people who knew Myra felt the same, but of course it was so much worse for John and his family.

I don't think you ever recover from something like that, but you have to deal with things, and I think Myra would be proud of the way John has dealt with things since her death.

I know he is proud and grateful for the part she played in his life.

Glenn Hoddle, summer 2008.

ACKNOWLEDGEMENTS

When I first started to think about putting my story into words I began to realise so many people had played a part in it, and I would like to thank each and every one of them.

Although I have managed to mention some of those who have touched my life, I realise I have not been able to record all of them, but that is always going to be the case with an autobiography and I hope they will accept my apologies. I have tried to tell my story in the best possible taste and to give a frank and honest account of what my life has been about.

I would like to thank Publisher Vanessa Gardner, Creative Director Kevin Gardner and all at Green Umbrella for their help and support in seeing this project through.

I would like to say a special thanks to Kevin Brennan who collaborated with me in the writing of this book, and to his wife Lynda and children James and Rachel. I have known Kevin for almost 30 years and nobody knows my story better than him. I also want to mention Myra's family and all of my nieces, nephews and friends, who have been so much part of my life over the years.

Finally, I want to give my biggest thanks to my children Amanda and Nick and to Rick, Jay and my wonderful grandchildren, Aaron and Josie.

John Gorman, summer 2008.

John Gorman

CHAPTER 1

Slipping Away

I had been at the club for a little less than four months and the boys were flying. We were in with a real chance of the play-offs, and everything seemed fantastic as I prepared the team for an away trip to Cambridge in mid-March 2005.

Wycombe was not a big club, but it was well run with fantastic people behind the scenes, great support and a real desire to get promotion from League Two. We had a terrific bunch of players and had edged our way up the table to ninth position. I was proud and pleased to be the manager, and had loved every minute since taking charge. After getting the sack at Tottenham it hadn't been easy finding a full-time job in the game again, but since being appointed as manager I'd very quickly felt at home. As far as I was concerned it was a smashing little club with real potential to progress and grow. I think we all felt we were moving in the right direction and although we were hardly awash with cash, the club tried to do the best they could to make sure I got the resources I needed.

Steve Hayes who had joined the board, and was clearly ambitious for the club, had suggested that I take the team away for a few days to Spain after the Cambridge game, and before the crucial Easter period that was coming up. After just one defeat in our last seven matches, things really couldn't have been better. It was a nice gesture and although it was only going to be for a few days, it was just the sort of break a team can do with before the final run-in to a tough season, and I knew it would also do no harm at all on the team spirit front. It wasn't a holiday, the players knew that they had to be professional about it and would be training each day we were there. But for a club like Wycombe it was a nice bonus for all of us and we were looking forward to it.

I got home from training feeling happy and full of enthusiasm for what was to come. My wife Myra had always shared in my footballing life. She wasn't the sort of wife who wasn't interested in the game, and had always been involved in everything I'd done, whether it was as a player, coach or manager. She'd been with me from my very first days at Celtic, and in the years that followed had to put up with an awful lot. She was always upbeat and always supportive. On more than one occasion as a player I'd gone off and signed for a new club leaving her to sort out everything else in our lives. It was alright for me, I would have my new club and team mates, but for Myra and other footballers' wives it wasn't quite the same, especially in those days when the money was nothing like it is today. One of her great qualities was that she was always upbeat and positive, but when I got home on this particular afternoon, I could sense something wasn't quite right.

GORY TALES

Myra eventually confided that she'd had stomach pains and had been feeling "a bit uncomfortable," as she put it. To most people this might not have been too much to worry about, but somehow at the back of both our minds alarm bells began to ring. The reason for this was the fact that Myra was in remission, having overcome breast cancer some years earlier. As far as we were concerned she'd beaten the disease, but there was something about the symptoms she described that made us both feel a bit uneasy.

She had already been to see her own GP, but he had virtually dismissed her concerns and pretty much said there was nothing for her to be worried about. Myra was hardly the sort of person to make a fuss, despite all she'd been through, but when I suggested that I would arrange for her to be seen by Gina Allan, who was the Wycombe club doctor, I think she was pleased and relieved.

Myra was happy for me to get on with the game at Cambridge, and straight after the match the party drove to Stansted Airport and flew off to Spain. The Cambridge match was a bit of a disaster and we looked flat, perhaps because the lads had their minds on the Spanish trip. Whatever the reason was, we certainly didn't do ourselves justice and ended up being beaten 2-1 by them. I had no idea that as we were travelling to stay in Cambridge on the Friday before the game, Myra was being seen by Gina. She hadn't told me about the appointment and, typically, didn't want to make a fuss about the whole thing. I later found out that Gina clearly thought there was a problem, because she quickly arranged for Myra to have a series of tests while I was away with the team in Spain.

We got back from the trip on a Wednesday and started preparing for the crucial home game against Northampton on Good Friday. It was actually on the day of the match that we got the results of the tests and discovered the cancer had returned. It was a huge blow but we were lucky and grateful that because of Gina, things had moved so quickly. We were due to play Northampton on the Friday evening and on the morning of the game, having got the news about the cancer, we found ourselves travelling to Harley Street in London for a first session with the specialist who had previously treated Myra. He was very positive and upbeat about her chances of beating the disease once again, but it was explained that she would have to start a series of treatment involving chemotherapy and radiotherapy, enduring all the side effects that come with it. Myra certainly wasn't frightened. She'd beaten it once and was determined to do it again. We also took heart from the confidence of the specialist, Peter Harper, who outlined what would happen to Myra, and ended by saying how optimistic he was about her coming through once again.

It was a tough day for her but she dealt with it all so well and wanted me to go off and take charge of the game against Northampton that evening. Their manager was Colin Calderwood, a good friend of ours, and someone who knew all about what Myra had gone through the first time around. He was really upset when I told him what had happened during the day, and the match took on a bit of a strange feel for me. We desperately wanted to win because Northampton were just a place above us in the table, but it proved to be another disappointment for us and we lost to the only goal of the game. We were never quite able to push on after that and failed to get into the play-off places as we'd hoped. It was a disappointment but it also made us all the more determined to make sure we succeeded the following season.

Since the diagnosis Myra had continued her fight to get rid of the cancer and my life had been all about trying to support and look after her, while at the same time act as manager of a football team. It's certainly the kind of duel role that takes its toll, but my problems were nothing compared to Myra's and, as strange as it might seem, you settle into a very different sort of routine which quickly becomes your everyday life.

Myra's treatment continued throughout the summer and everything was looking good. We were being told she was doing well. She'd had chemotherapy and radiotherapy before and knew what to expect. She never once moaned even though it must be absolutely horrible for people who have to go through it. One of the side effects was hair loss, but we got her a wig and she just used to laugh the whole thing off. She had such a great spirit and never allowed anyone to feel sorry for her.

We even managed to get away to Spain that summer for a few days with our great friends Tommy and Margaret Cannon, and on one occasion the positive feedback we were getting from the specialist prompted Myra and I to go for a glass of champagne after a hospital visit. It was actually the day of the London bombings in July 2005, and sitting at the table next to us were a couple of girls who had been caught up in it all earlier in the day. It must have been traumatic for them and I suppose all four of us were sitting there thinking just how precious life was.

We never really had any kind of time scale when it came to Myra. She just continued her treatment and we got on with our lives. Of course it was difficult, but at the same time, the last thing you can do in a situation like that is to stop doing the normal things. If anything it certainly helped me to have all the pre-season preparations to take care of with Wycombe.

The team started the new campaign in tremendous form and we quickly began to climb up the league. By mid-December we had gone 21 games without defeat and were top of the table. Things were going great for me as a manager, but it was clear by now that Myra's battle was beginning to take its toll.

John Gorman

The club had been fantastically supportive right from the very start, and had tried to make life easier in whatever way they could. Steve Hayes arranged for Myra to have a car take her up to London for treatment, and I used to drive up and meet her at the hospital after taking training. It was a routine we soon got into and there were still positive noises coming from the specialist.

But by the time December had arrived there was a definite change in Myra. For the first time she looked as though she was being worn down by the fight she was so bravely staging. I suppose the change was a gradual one in many ways, which probably started around September time.

She brightened up with the visit of Sue Gunn, one of our great friends from America. We had got to know Sue and her husband Bill from our time in Arizona, when I played in Phoenix, and she came to visit us early in January. Myra clearly wanted to show Sue all sorts of places, and it was good for her to have a friend over, even though I could see the strain of the disease taking its toll. Sue was still with us one Saturday when I got a call at about 10.30 in the morning. Wycombe were top of the league at the time and we were due to play Notts County at home that afternoon. The date was 14 January 2006 and it was a day which began one of the saddest and most difficult periods of my life.

The call was bad news. It was to tell me that one of my young players, Mark Philo, had been involved in a car accident and was in a really bad way. I raced over to the hospital in Reading where he had been taken after the crash and immediately began to realise just how serious things were. His mum Christine and dad, Pas, were there and I was told that it was pretty much a hopeless case. Poor Mark was only being kept alive by a life-support machine.

GORY TALES

It was truly horrific. The poor kid was only 21-years-old and had been at the club since he was 15. He was a really talented midfielder and although he'd had some injury problems, a lot was expected of him and there were high hopes that he would go on to make a top player. The other real tragedy to come out of this was the fact that the accident had also killed a 47-year-old woman, Trisha Gammon who, like Myra at the time, was due to soon have a grandchild born. With the game coming up in the afternoon I didn't know what to do. I suppose my first instincts were to have the match called-off, but Mark's parents actually told me they wanted the game to go ahead and that we should play it for him.

It was such a strange experience. On the one hand I felt as though I should be at the hospital, but there I was thinking ahead to the game and trying to work out how we could play the match. It was all very surreal. I spoke to Steve Hayes and the club secretary Keith Allen. Keith's immediate reaction was to say the fixture should be cancelled, but then I told him how Mark's parents wanted us to go ahead with it and win the game for their son. After speaking to Steve again and the club chairman, Ivor Beeks, we decided to carry on with the match. I shared the news about Mark with my assistant manager, Steve Brown, but not my coaches, Keith Ryan and Jim Barron and none of the players knew about what had happened. Perhaps some of them might have expected Mark to be there, but in the end they probably thought he had a touch of flu or some other minor complaint, so there was never a suspicion that something more serious might have happened.

We played the match and won it 2-0, it was a horrible wet day and after the final whistle blew, I got the team in a huddle and told them I had something to tell them when we got back into the dressing room. I said I was warning them on the pitch because I didn't want it to hit them hard when we got inside. They all knew about Myra and instinctively thought it was something to do with her, but moments later they discovered it wasn't.

Mark had actually passed away during the game when the life-support machine was switched off, and the club got a call to say what had happened. By the time I got the team back in the dressing room the directors were there as well and we had all the backroom staff associated with the side including medical people who I knew would have a role to play once I broke the news to the players. Telling them was a terrible experience. There were people crying and almost screaming with grief and disbelief when I told them what had happened. It was horrible, truly horrible and no matter what experience you've had in the game as a coach or manager, nothing can prepare you for a moment like that. It was clear that everyone in that dressing room needed each other at that moment, because the whole thing was so difficult to comprehend. A young boy who was popular and with his whole life in front of him – gone.

Tragedy is an over-used word in football. A player gets an injury that keeps him out of action for a few weeks; a penalty is missed; a team dominates a game and then concedes a last minute penalty. How many times have you heard instances like that described as a tragedy? But when you experience true tragedy as everyone in that dressing room did, it has a numbing effect. Nobody quite knew how to deal with the news. I felt as manager that I had to show some leadership and help everyone as best I could to deal with the situation, even though I was probably as stunned as them. The whole club was in shock and in the days that followed time seemed to stand still as we tried to carry on as best we could.

I was also very much aware that poor Mark wasn't the only one who had died, and I made it my business to quickly find out about the woman who had lost her life in the crash. Her death was horrific enough but discovering that her daughter was due to give birth at virtually the same time as our own Amanda, made the whole thing seem a lot more personal to us. It was terrible to think about what her poor family must have been going through and I wasn't sure they'd actually want to hear from me, but they were marvellous. I sent flowers and met her son-in-law, who was very understanding and could see how concerned I was for them as well.

Mark's funeral was on the Thursday following the crash, and the church at Crowthorne was absolutely packed. There were people standing in the street outside as the service took place and as well as his friends and family there were also a lot of football people there. It was a terribly sad day for everyone and I don't think his death and the crash had really sunk in when the team took to the field at Barnet two days after the funeral to play a league game. We somehow managed to get a 0-0 draw, but looking back at it now, I'm sure our minds were not fully concentrated on the match. Young players in the squad like Jonny Dixon and Russell Martin, were very close to Mark, but I think it also affected more experienced players like skipper Roger Johnson, Tommy Mooney and former England midfielder Rob Lee. We all knew that the following day the club were going to hold a memorial service for Mark at the ground. That was obviously another emotionally charged moment in what had been such a difficult week for everyone to cope with. I gave a speech which allowed me to talk about Mark and what a loss his death was. The fans came along to the service and there was a real outpouring of feeling. I think it helped in many ways for lots of people to get some sort of closure over such a sad event which had touched so many, even those who didn't really know the boy.

The very next day Myra and I went along to the funeral of Trisha Gammon.

John Gorman

I had asked the permission of her family because I wasn't sure they would want me there, but they were very good about the whole thing and said it would be alright for me to go along. I found it all very sad and very moving, so much so that I suddenly found myself crying during the service. I think it was the emotion of the past 10 days and the fact that somehow it struck a chord with me. She would have been looking forward to a new grandchild, and now she was dead. I think I saw some similarity in her situation and Myra's. Thoughts of birth and death were lurking in my mind making it a very emotionally charged moment for me.

By this time Myra really wasn't very well at all, although I was still unaware of quite how ill she was and the fact that the cancer was taking more of a grip. I was still running around like a lunatic, trying to do my job as a manager, with the club still in mourning because of what had happened to poor Mark. At the same time my wife was clearly suffering and she started to take a turn for the worse at the end of January.

It was crazy really because at the time I was putting a lot of energy into trying to persuade Jermaine Easter to sign for us in an £80,000 deal from Stockport, with the club having just sold Nathan Tyson to Nottingham Forest for £600,000. It was the end of the transfer window and eventually Jermaine signed for us. Transfers can be time consuming and a lot of hours are put in trying to get everything done and sorted out. Just as all of this was going on Myra began to feel a change in her condition. Her body was beginning to swell and she immediately contacted Gina. She was told that she would have to have excess fluid drained from her, but Myra was still allowed to stay at home and despite all that was going on, we were both optimistic that it was just another hurdle she was going to be able to overcome.

However, things changed dramatically soon after that. While I was away with the team for a match at Wrexham early in February, Myra was being taken to Harley Street by our next door neighbour, Paula Bury, who along with her husband, Richard, had become great friends of ours. On the morning of the match I got a call from the specialist and for the first time his mood had changed. The optimism that had previously been there on our past visits had suddenly disappeared. He told me he wanted to be honest with me and that things were not looking good. They were trying to keep the swelling down, but it was a difficult process as they continued to drain fluid from her swelling body.

Things began to get worse by the hour in many ways. I still had to try and juggle being manager and being Myra's husband. On one terrible occasion I came off the training pitch to be told that my kids, Nick and Amanda, had been trying to get hold of me because Myra had undergone an emergency operation. It was literally a life or death situation and she'd had to have an operation on her throat together with a transfusion after losing a massive amount of blood.

Myra was put into intensive care and while she was moved there I ended up sleeping in the hospital bed in her private room each night, before driving back to take training. It was stupid really and nobody at the club was forcing me to do it, I just felt it was something I should be doing. But things got pretty bad and in the end I missed our home game with Mansfield because there was no way I was going to be away with her in such a poor condition.

Somehow Myra managed to recover from that set-back and she was trying to put a brave face on everything, she even encouraged me to go to the following game at Notts County a few days later, but I wasn't about to take the team. I just drove up there and sat in the stand. Although she must have been feeling awful Myra was clearly thinking about me, and I believe she told

John Gorman

me to go because she wanted to try and take my mind off things a little. It was an amazing thing to do and once again showed the sort of person she was. I went to the next game as well, which was at Boston. I didn't go with the team, but chairman Ivor Beeks picked me up and I watched as we battered them but only picked up a 1-1 draw. In the previous few days Myra's body had been swelling up and her legs were bruised, but she just made fun of it and carried on showing that fantastic spirit which had got her through so much. She wanted things to carry on as normally as possible. My son Nick and his fiancé Jay had planned a trip to Thailand for him to meet her parents. He was reluctant to go because of his mother's condition, but the medical staff assured us it would be fine, and so they went ahead a couple of days before that Boston game. When I got back from the match I went straight to the hospital and as I walked through the door to Myra's room her sister Eileen was with her. Something told me she wasn't right. Soon after she was moved to intensive care and once again I stayed in her bed at the hospital so that I could be near her. At about five in the morning early on the Monday an Irish nurse who had been helping to look after Myra came into the room and woke me up. It was pretty clear she was concerned as she explained why she had woken me.

"I know your son is in Thailand," she said. "But if I were you I'd get him back."

The look on her face said it all and I rushed up to the intensive care unit to see Myra. You didn't have to be a medical expert to know she had taken a real turn for the worse. Her eyes were sunken and red. She really looked as though the suffering was overwhelming her. There were nurses there and I think they could see how shocked and upset I was by what I saw. One of the younger ones began to cry. She had seen the deterioration and there was clearly no point in anyone trying to hide the truth. She tried to explain things in layman's terms for me and basically said that Myra's body was giving out on her. There was no chance of her being able to win this latest battle.

"Does that mean she's going to die?" I asked.

The nurse, who was still very emotional about what was happening, nodded. "Yes," she said. "I'm afraid it does."

"Well she's not dying here," I told her trying to hold back my own tears. "I want her to come home."

All the medical staff clearly understood my feelings, and had no problem with what I had in mind, so arrangements were made for Myra to leave the hospital and spend the last days of her life in the home we had both come to love so much. After so many moves it was the place we felt most comfortable. We had put down roots and had great friends in the area. I knew that bringing her home was the right thing to do. The people in the hospital had been tremendous and the nurses couldn't have done more for her, but I just had a very strong feeling about it and knew that was where Myra wanted to be.

We got her home and with the help of the MacMillan nurses who were with her around the clock, things were made as comfortable as possible. In fact, she was actually able to talk to people who came to visit. She was heavily drugged in an effort to numb the pain, but in many ways it was all quite peaceful. We had music playing in the background all the time and although everyone knew that the inevitable was going to happen, at least a horrible situation was somehow made better. Nick had returned from Thailand, and Amanda was there. Myra's sisters, Eileen and Joan and her brother, Ian, also came down, as did Tommy Cannon.

One of the great pleasures for Myra during all of her pain was the fact that she managed to see and hold her new granddaughter, Josie, who had been

John Gorman

born the day after I had gone to the Notts County game. Myra had been due to be the birth mother for Amanda but was too ill to be there, so her sister Eileen stood in. Amanda realised how bad things were getting and was desperate for her mum to see the baby, so she was induced. I will never forget the day we got the news about Josie being born. Myra was actually walking with the aid of a Zimmer frame in hospital at the time, and she'd gone to the toilet when the phone rang. It was Amanda's husband, Rick, with the news that we'd become grandparents for a second time and that our grandson, Aaron, now had a little sister. The sheer look of joy on Myra's face when I told her the news was unbelievable. It's a look I will never forget. She was so happy and relieved that she had been spared long enough to see the baby. I went straight from Myra's bed to see Amanda in hospital. The next day Amanda made sure she was out and on her way to see Myra. That morning we had a picture taken with Myra holding the baby, and you can see what it meant to her and how it lifted all of our spirits at the time.

Although I was pleased that we managed to get Myra home for what I knew would be the final few days of her life. I can't pretend it wasn't upsetting. I could see her slowly but surely getting worse, and despite all the drugs and the wonderful care she got from the nurses, it was just a terrible time. The worst thing was that I actually found myself wanting her to pass away. I didn't want her to have to endure the sort of agony she must have been going through.

She had arrived back at the house on a Monday, and by the end of the week I was told it would be just a matter of time, and that the end might come over the weekend. I sat with her on the Saturday and, strange as it may sound, there I was listening to commentary of Wycombe's home game with Oxford. I still felt responsible for the team as well. It was a weird feeling. Here was my wife lying there dying, I was holding her hand and she was squeezing mine, but at the same time I was listening to the match. I was worrying about the team as well which was crazy, because in the circumstances it just didn't matter.

Myra died the next night. It was odd because although the house was full of family, they were out of the room at the time. It was just me and Jay who was making tea. She was on one side of the bed and I was on the other. I just looked at Myra and knew. I knew she was taking her last breath on this earth. I called out and the room was quickly full of people. We were all there as Myra's suffering finally ended.

The funeral followed four days later. The service was conducted by Father Mike Hoare, who had also given Myra the last rites and was wonderful to us throughout a very difficult period. The church was absolutely packed. I wanted it to be a celebration of Myra's life and that's what it turned out to be. It was full of the people who had been a part of her life, and as sad as it was for all of us, I think her beautiful spirit shone through the ceremony. It was such a strange experience for me and it was as if it was all happening to someone else. It took weeks before the full impact of what had happened finally hit me. The enormity of losing the person who had always been there, the woman I'd been in love with since we were little more than kids. My darling Myra was gone.

CHAPTER 2

FOOTBALL CRAZY

It was love at first sight. Pure and simple as far as I was concerned, as soon as Myra walked through the door that was it.

The place was a village hall and it was 1967. We were both 17-year-olds and I had gone there to help my friend Jim Campbell celebrate his 21st birthday. Like quite a few mates of mine at that time, he was a bit older than me but it made no difference. We had known each other for years and playing football had been the common thread that had bound us all together.

We all came from roughly the same area and something like a 21st birthday party was pretty big news. Word had got around that there were a couple of girls coming along who were not really local and I certainly didn't know them, but when I saw Myra that night it was amazing. I knew she was the one for me as stupid as it may sound, and it wasn't long before I introduced myself. Much to my relief it seemed as though she liked me too and we hit it off right from the word go.

Shortly after that party we started dating and I would regularly cycle the 12 miles from my house to her home near Edinburgh to see her. I was a young footballer playing for Celtic, the club of my dreams, and it didn't take me long to realise just what a lucky boy I was because I knew I had met the girl of my dreams as well. Sounds corny I know, but that was how I felt. I couldn't have been happier. Although I have to admit, I never dreamed back then that I would be with her for another 39 years. I think it was somehow meant to be and I always say that Jim's 21st turned out to be the best party I ever went to, because that was where I met Myra.

She very quickly became a part of my life and the great thing was that she really liked her football and was always encouraging me in my career, something she continued to do until the day she died. Back then I was really football crazy. My life revolved around the game and had done for as long as I could remember.

I came from a very ordinary working class background and lived in what was then the village of Winchburgh in West Lothian. We were nearer to Edinburgh than Glasgow, but when it came to football teams there was only ever one mentioned in our house – Celtic. My dad, Bernard, and older brother, Joseph, were both fanatics and it didn't take me long to follow in their footsteps. I loved my football and soon realised I had a talent for the game. As far as I was concerned I knew from a very early age just what I wanted to be, and that was a professional footballer. Of course, I was hardly alone in that ambition and I reckon most of the boys in our village had the same idea. Somewhere along the way a lot of them found their dreams and aspirations changing, but I never did. I had some luck, and I needed to have footballing talent, but what I also had in abundance was determination. I was so focused on achieving my goal, even though I'm sure a lot of people just saw me as a football mad kid.

Pretty much everything I did seemed to revolve around the game and I was never very far from a football. We lived at number 127 Millgate and my granny Rosanne lived up the hill at number one. She was my mother Annie's mum and I was always very close to her and also to my aunt Mary.

My gran was a lovely lady and lived to the ripe old age of 96. Four years before her death she had flown for the very first time and made a trip across the Atlantic to come and see me play for Tampa Bay Rowdies in Florida. She was a real character and everyone over there loved her. They even gave her the nickname of granny Rowdie!

When I was a small boy and my mum was out at work I would be given the task of going up to my gran's and collecting the food for the meal in the evening. It always seemed to be some form of meat with potatoes to go along with it. "Meat and Tatties" were pretty popular, except on Friday when, being Catholics, we would swap the usual for fish and chips. The pots and dishes containing the food would be pretty heavy, especially for a small boy like me, but I would set myself a task whenever I went to collect the food. I would hold the pots and pans, and at the same time I'd be juggling a football. I used to love juggling with both feet and although there were a couple of accidents along the way when I dropped the pots, most of the time I was successful at playing "Keepie Uppie" while at the same time delivering the food for our dinner table. It became a bit of a personal challenge for me and I loved it. Anything to do with a football and I was in my element.

One of my great pals at the time was a slightly older lad named Tommy Cannon, who as I've mentioned, is still a dear friend to this day, and when we were both kids he would really encourage me with my football. He'd spend hours with me helping to improve my skill and ability with the ball. He even had the patience to stand by and count how many times I could keep the ball in the air, using one foot and then the other. It would go on for ages some times, but Tommy was always prepared to count and encourage me. I owe him a lot and he was not only a good friend, he would often act as a wise older head. I could be a bit reckless as a kid and I was always getting myself into scrapes. My brother Joseph would often come to my rescue, and Tommy was the one who usually made sure I got up to nothing more harmful than kicking a football around. Unfortunately, when I was nine-years-old Tommy wasn't around on one particular summer's night when a prank with some of my other mates ended with me almost losing my life.

It was innocent enough and all about boys of that age doing what they do best, and that is getting into mischief. As a young lad I was a little bit wild. Not a bad kid, but the sort of boy who would be happiest playing with my mates. Most times that meant nothing more dangerous than playing football, but on this particular occasion we had all decided to put the ball to one side and investigate a building site in the village. They were constructing new houses there and it was the perfect adventure playground as far as we were concerned. Once the builders had all gone off home, we moved in and began to muck around. None of the houses had been fully completed and they were all just shells really, but great fun to clamber about in and I soon found myself climbing one of them with some of my mates. We were on the roof mucking about when suddenly one of the bricks gave way. They had all been cemented that afternoon and hadn't quite set properly. I went flying through the air and crashed to the ground.

What made matters worse was the fact that I fell onto a pile of bricks making my landing bumpy to say the least. In fact, I was in absolute agony and my left arm was virtually cut in half and hanging by a thread. The whole thing must have looked pretty bad because the arm got bent behind my back and there was blood everywhere.

I was in terrible pain and one of my friends somehow managed to help me get back to my own house. I'd lost a lot of blood by then and my poor mother had the shock of her life when she saw me come staggering through the door, my arm dangling limply at my side, with blood running all over the floor from my wound.

"Jesus, Mary and Joseph!" she screamed as she saw me. It was particularly shocking for her because she thought I was at our local church going to benediction, so to see me in such a state must have been horrific. Not surprisingly, she panicked but then had the presence of mind to run to one of our neighbours, Mrs Campbell, who was a nurse. She came rushing back to the house and took charge. Quite a few people later said she probably saved my life and I was certainly in a really poor state. Things were so bad that a priest was called and he gave me the last rites, because they honestly thought that not only my arm, but also my life was hanging by a thread.

It was the loss of blood which caused most concern and although I was in terrible pain I suppose I was oblivious to all the panic that was going on around me. When I finally got to a hospital they managed to get things under control and my condition began to stabilise. It was obviously a worrying time for my mum and dad and a very painful one for me. I ended up staying in hospital for quite a while, much of it with my arm in plaster, but even then football was never very far from my thoughts. I used to get some very strange looks from the staff as I maintained my juggling with a football, despite the plaster! My arm eventually healed, but the accident did leave me with a permanent problem. To this day I still can't straighten it fully, and as a player I was never able to take a long throw-in. The funny thing was that up to that point, I still had ambitions of maybe playing in goal, but the injury put paid to all of that, although years later when I was playing indoor soccer in the States I did actually get to play between the sticks.

Winchburgh was a lovely little place and I had a very contented childhood. There wasn't too much there when I was growing up and like so many places it has expanded over the years, but when I was a kid it had a lovely cosy feel to it. There were a couple of pubs, a bakers, an ice cream shop, all the sort of things you would associate with a village in that part of the world. There were plenty of places to play as well, with a couple of castles, Niddry and Duntarvie near by, which we used as playgrounds, climbing all over the place. We also had a patch of land where we'd play football surrounded by the shale slag heaps or "bings" as they were called, from the mines which closed when I was about 12-years-old. Although Winchburgh was a small place it did manage to produce quite a few lads who went on to make their name by playing football. People like goalkeeper Willie Harper who played for Scotland, Willie Thornton, who played for Rangers, Jimmy Scouler, Willie Duff and Davie Gibson, who played for his country and also had a very successful career with Leicester and Aston Villa in England.

One of my favourite past times as a kid was playing football with my mates in front of our houses. The homes were all next door to each other and the area was shaped like an old three penny bit. We each had a gate in front of the entrance to the house and that acted as our own personal goal. We'd have to try and protect our own goal while at the same time trying to kick the ball through one of our opponent's gates.

I had a lot of freedom to go out and play with my friends, and a great

John Gorman

family life, with mum, dad and my brother as well as my granddad and granny, who I was very close to. There wasn't much money about, but there was always enough and both of my parents worked hard to make sure we had a comfortable and secure existence. Dad had been in the Black Watch during the Second World War and had twice been taken prisoner. Everyone said that he came back a changed man, which is no surprise when you think about it. By the time I arrived he was working in the building trade doing things like plastering and mum was a typist. She was also a very talented singer and it was a shame that she never got the chance to take her love of music further. She clearly had an artistic streak and quite apart from the music, I remember that she had great handwriting as well and that side of her character seemed to get passed down to both Joseph and me. We both loved our art and he would paint some great landscapes. I favoured portrait painting, but over the years I've tried my hand at all sorts of things and apart from my football, art has always been something that has been there and remained a very important part of my life. I would always be drawing and painting at home, but never had any formal training as a kid. It was just something I did as a hobby and the enjoyment has lasted to this day. It has always come easily to me and as well as the pure pleasure I get from painting and drawing, I also find it a great way to relax.

We were very much a Catholic family and both my mum and dad were religious, my mum particularly so. But I had loads of friends who were Protestant and religion was never a problem growing up in Winchburgh. Football was something that united so many of the kids living there.

Celtic was the other religion, certainly for my dad and brother. Both of them were fanatical in their support and although they didn't go to every game, they seemed to have green and white blood running through their veins. Supporting Celtic seemed like second nature as far as I was concerned and it wasn't long before I was getting a taste of the atmosphere as my dad and brother took me along to some home games. The first time I set foot in Celtic Park I thought the atmosphere was magical. The noise was deafening and the crowd was huge. In those days it was all about standing and watching your football, because there were no all-seater stadiums, but that just seemed to add to the magic. It was a special place and it made me even more determined to fulfil my dream of becoming a professional footballer.

Schoolwork always had to play second fiddle to my football, I was pretty average when it came to all the academic stuff, but I did love sport and in particular football. I also enjoyed doing my art, but when it came to the big question that all kids were asked at one stage or another by the headmaster, there was only one answer. What did I want to be when I left school? That was easy. I wanted to be a footballer. I'd get the usual knowing smile because so many boys would say the same, but from a very early age I had tremendous self-belief. It wasn't just the fact that I could do my juggling and feel comfortable with a football, I also played regularly for teams, and it would often be for sides with much older boys in them. I knew I could hold my own in that sort of company and if I could have played matches 24 hours a day that would have suited me fine, because I was totally besotted with the game.

By the time I was 13-years-old I had started playing for a local team called Uphall Saints, who were an under-16's side. They had some very good young players in their side, boys who were county players and there were often professional scouts sniffing around at various matches keeping their eyes on people who might have the potential to make it with league clubs. Although I'd gone all the way through to the final Scottish trials, I'd just failed to get selected, but the process helped to confirm to me that I could play and compete with some of the best youngsters in the country.

Uphall had a couple of players in the side called Joe McGrath and Peter Duncan, both were very talented and had played for Scotland schoolboys. One day before a match we heard that there was a Celtic scout due to come and have a look at the game. It was supposed to be Sean Fallon who wanted to run the rule over McGrath and Duncan, but on the day he didn't turn up and instead it was a guy called John Higgins who was there to take a look at the pair. After the match our coach, Bill Kelly, pulled me to one side.

"There's been a Celtic scout here today," he told me.

Like lots of the other lads in the team I'd heard the rumour about Celtic being interested in McGrath, who was a really strong midfielder and clearly looked as though he had a future in the game, but then Kelly took the wind out of my sails with his next comment.

"He was impressed with Duncan and with you," he said. "He wants you to go for a trial with Celtic John."

CHAPTER 3

LIVING THE DREAM

I couldn't wait to get home and tell my dad and brother the news. I knew they would be as thrilled as I was, but I had a hard time convincing them the whole thing was true.

"Are you sure you don't mean Linlithgo Celtic, or Blantyre Celtic?" my dad asked. There were quite a few local amateur teams who had the name "Celtic" tagged on and he was convinced it must have been one of them who had a scout at our game.

"No dad," I told him. "It was someone from THE Celtic. Glasgow Celtic!"

I could see he thought I'd got the wrong end of the stick, but at the same time dad went along with it, not wanting to disappoint me by saying anything. But a few days later he realised I'd got it right and nobody could have been happier than him when the letter arrived confirming exactly what I had told him. It was a wonderful moment for me as I held the letter with the famous Celtic crest at the top of the page. I knew it could be the chance I needed to begin my career as a footballer and I was determined to make the most of it.

When the day came for the trial I just couldn't wait to show what I could do. To be honest, getting to Celtic that day was a bit of a trial in itself because, as I've mentioned, we lived more than 40 miles away from the ground so it wasn't just a case of popping around the corner. There were buses and a train journey involved but I was convinced it would all be worth it once I got there.

Celtic have always been a massive club and back then, even though they weren't top dogs in Scotland, with Rangers the more successful outfit, they were still able to attract some of the best players around and had their pick of all the promising youngsters who were coming through. When I got to the ground there were loads of other kids hanging around waiting for their chance to show what they could do as well, and they all looked a lot older than me. I was as nervous as anything and the butterflies were playing havoc with my stomach, so much so that for a while I just couldn't stop breaking wind. In fact, because I was just 13 I shouldn't really have been involved in a trial, but that didn't seem to matter too much, although I did have to play under an assumed name as I was put in a team that took on a Scottish under-17 side. I can't remember the score, but I do remember that I played in what was my usual position at the time, which was left-half. I must have done all right, because they asked me to start training with them on a regular basis, making that long journey to Glasgow twice a week.

I was too young to sign as a schoolboy because you had to be 15-years-old to do that, but as far as I was concerned I was on my way. I was living the dream of taking my first steps on the ladder to becoming a professional player, and it was incredibly exciting.

GORY TALES

I was as mad as ever about the game and just couldn't get enough football. Whether it was watching Celtic with my dad and brother, training with them twice a week or playing with my own side Uphall Saints. It was all football and I loved it. Finishing school couldn't come quickly enough for me. Don't get me wrong, I wasn't one of those boys who hated it with a passion, but I had a one-track mind and all my thoughts were on playing football rather than studying.

The training sessions with Celtic were great and I used to really look forward to them. Tommy Cannon, would go with me most times and he was always encouraging me. There seemed to be loads of kids training during those sessions and that was when I first came across another boy who later went on to make a big name for himself with Celtic, Scotland and Chelsea and would become a lifelong friend of mine. His name was David Hay, and I could see from very early on that he had great skill, and was as determined as I was to make the grade. We would all be training behind the goals at Celtic Park, which was a thrill in itself, but it also gave us the chance to polish up our skills with the ball and take part in training sessions with other boys who were clearly talented footballers. We also made use of the running track and the car park outside the ground. It was great, we were all there on merit, and all after the same thing, but only a very small percentage of the players who passed through the club at that time would actually go on to make it and be signed on by Celtic. Of course, none of us even thought along those lines, we were just pleased to be out there each week.

Although I had my trial when I was 13, I didn't actually start training with Celtic until I was 14, and for a whole year after that I knew that I had to impress the people who would be making the decision about whether to sign me on schoolboy forms. Happily, when the time came I got the nod and was

John Gorman

taken on. It was a great feeling to be part of such a fantastic club, and a thrill to be signed by Jimmy McGrory, who was a real Celtic legend. He was a great goalscorer in his day, getting 50 in one season, and still holds the record for the most goals scored for the club with a total of 397.

But if Jimmy was a Celtic legend already when I signed for them as a schoolboy, the club were soon to be managed by a man who would also achieve legendary status during his time. Jock Stein took over as manager from Jimmy in March 1965, and he went on to achieve so much during his time in charge. Big Jock was a dominating and intimidating figure for a youngster like me, but he was certainly not a bully or someone who would rant and rave for the sake of it. He just had great presence and an authority about him. He had the air of a man who knew exactly how he wanted things done and he very quickly became Mr Celtic, with little going on at the club that he did not have an influence on.

Even when it came to the youngsters, big Jock had rules that had to be adhered to. He was a great believer in the kids getting a trade behind them, and not just relying on making the grade as a footballer. He knew there were so many kids who would have their dreams shattered and for many of them there was no way of getting another club. It meant their hopes of earning a living from the game could simply disappear and without a trade to fall back on they might struggle. It was very forward-thinking really and probably something I should have been grateful for, but when I found out what was arranged for me, my happiness at leaving school and signing for Celtic started to disappear.

One of the Celtic directors, Mr Thomas Devlin, owned a trawler firm in Edinburgh and it was decided that I should go and work for them, thankfully not actually going to sea, but learning my trade as a carpenter. It was a bit of a nightmare from the first day I arrived. The guy I was told to work with had a drink problem and you could smell the booze on his breath at eight in the morning.

The stench on the boats was terrible as well, and I knew from the first moment that the whole thing wasn't for me. The guy with the drink problem actually dropped dead in front of me one day, which was a pretty harrowing experience. I really didn't enjoy being there but stuck it out for about six months before summoning the courage to have a word with big Jock about the way I was feeling. To be fair to him, he was very understanding, and I think the fact that I had been making good progress and getting involved regularly, meant that he was prepared to make the decision to take me onto the groundstaff.

I was in a funny situation in many ways, because although I was attached to Celtic, I was not a full-time professional and I was still playing local football as well. In fact, I was in demand when it came to the local amateur clubs and they were all quite famous. They had some very good players in their teams, and one of the clubs called Edina Hibs, were constantly after signing me. The guy who ran it actually came to my house in an effort to get me to play for them, but I stayed loyal to Uphall and continued playing my football with them.

Edina were a very good side and had a lot of success. They played to a very high standard and were excellent to watch. They reached the final of a local cup competition and the match was due to be played at Tynecastle, the home of Hearts in Edinburgh. I arranged to meet my dad there so that we could watch the game together along with the Uphall coach.

It was at the time when I was working at the trawler company and just before being taken onto the groundstaff, I got the bus into Edinburgh and then ran all the way to the ground, which was a distance of just under two miles. I was as fit as a fiddle and loved running, but I don't quite know why I raced to Tynecastle that night, I just remember wanting to get to the ground as quickly as I could. When I did get there the first person I saw was the guy who ran the Edina team, the same man who had tried to get me to play for them.

"Would you like to play for us tonight John?" he asked.

"Yeah," I said without hesitation. The thought of playing in a cup final in front of a decent crowd and at the home of a professional football club was just too good to resist. I was still in my working clothes, but he wasn't put off by the fact that I had no playing gear with me and after ushering me into the dressing room, he proceeded to find a pair of boots for me. They must have belonged to one of the other kids, but I didn't care where they came from, as long as they fitted I was happy to wear them and even happier to run out onto the pitch and hear the roar of the crowd.

My dad certainly wasn't making any noise at that point because he was left speechless when he saw me running out in the colours of Edina, although my Uphall coach wasn't as quiet and let rip with a stream of expletives when he saw what had happened. Neither of them could believe it, but I was absolutely delighted to be taking part in such a big match. It didn't seem to matter that I'd never played for Edina before and that I was an Uphall player, to me it was all about the football and the lure of playing in a big cup final.

Edina won the game but my euphoria disappeared a few days later when I found out that I had been given a one year ban from playing matches because I'd competed as an unregistered player for them. It was a bitter blow for me, especially as things had been going so well. I was still able to train with Celtic, but I wasn't allowed to play in any matches, competitive or friendly games.

GORY TALES

At first I thought they would just make an example of me and then forget about the whole thing after a few weeks, but the ban went on for months and eventually it took the intervention of Jock Stein to get it lifted. He argued that all I'd ever wanted to do was play football, which was absolutely true, and I was finally allowed to play in matches again.

Being able to play once more was fantastic and when I did come back I went and played for Edina because it was such a good standard of football, but I made sure I signed all the right forms first! In fact, I signed provisional forms for Celtic in October 1964, when I was 15, but although I was on the club's books I was still allowed to play for Edina as well because I wasn't a full-time professional. At the time Celtic were beginning to assemble one of the greatest teams in the club's history, but it wasn't just the first team that was strong. Celtic only had three teams, but the quality of players they could pick from was incredible. They undoubtedly had the best footballers on offer in Scotland and the third team regularly had about 30 players waiting to see which of them had made the starting line-up, which illustrates just how strong they were.

There is often a lot made about the part religion has played when it comes to football in Glasgow. Celtic has always been seen as the Catholic club and Rangers the Protestant side. But although Celtic always seemed to mop up the best of the Catholic players, there were also a lot of Protestant footballers there as well when I joined. Big Jock himself was a Protestant and as far as he was concerned religion didn't come into the equation, it was all about football and nothing else mattered, which is exactly how it should be in my opinion. The other thing to remember is that some of the greatest players Celtic have had in their history have not been Catholics. Just think of names like Willie Wallace, Tommy Gemmell and Bertie Auld. I had great friends who were there with me when I joined, people like Kenny Dalglish and Danny McGrain, both of whom were Protestants. There was never any animosity between the players and it worked well for Celtic. There was occasionally a bit of good natured banter, but that was all it was and there certainly weren't any bigots in the club. You were there because you wanted to play for Celtic, pure and simple. The club was bigger than any individual and we were all well aware of that.

When you were taken on as a groundstaff boy in those days it wasn't all about playing football. You were pretty much the lowest of the low when it came to the pecking order which meant that as well as training and playing matches, you were also expected to help carry out all the menial chores at the club. I soon got used to cleaning boots as well as painting and sweeping the terraces. But probably the worst part was washing out the toilets, especially after there had been a big match the previous Saturday with thousands of people at the ground. It was also pretty hard work cleaning up after a big Celtic-Rangers encounter, with broken bottles scattered all over the terraces and the stench of urine constantly in the air as you went about your job. The famous "jungle" terrace at Celtic Park had been somewhere I'd stood to watch my heroes, I never thought at the time that I'd to be cleaning it one day!

I very quickly made some great friends at the club and also realised just how good the players were. The reserve team that I got into had some truly tremendous kids in it, and some of them would go on to play a big part in the club's history and become household names in the game. That second team actually got the nickname of the "Quality Street Kids," because it contained so many talented youngsters. We knew we were good and there was real competition for places. Things were a bit different back then and playing in the reserves for a few seasons was an accepted part of your football education. With very few exceptions you just didn't get youngsters bursting onto the scene and forcing their way straight into the first team. Playing in the Celtic first team was something that only happened after a period of years and then only if you were very good or very lucky. Players had to bide their time and be prepared to wait. It was frustrating up to a point, but then you looked at the lads who were in the team and really there was no argument.

To get into the reserves was an achievement in itself and there were some great names that I played alongside and who would regularly turn out for the second team. Players like John Fallon, Danny McGrain, David Hay, George Connelly, David Cattanach, Kenny Dalglish who was playing in midfield at that time, Jimmy Quinn and Lou Macari. Quite often we would also get some of the more experienced players coming into the side as well when they were not on first team duty. We would play in front of some big crowds and there were games against other club's first teams. I actually remember going to Brunton Park, a place I would later come to know very well, to play against Carlisle, and we beat them.

There were some great characters at the club and none more so than Big Jock himself. On one particular occasion the reserves were playing in a League Cup competition. It was our last game and in order to qualify and finish above Rangers in our section, we had to beat Partick Thistle by seven clear goals. Jock always had a way of making an entrance. He didn't just walk through the door he would come bursting in! Sure enough, on this particular day the door flew open and the big man came straight to the point.

"Right lads, you've got to win this by seven clear goals," he said. "Do that and there's a wee bonus for you."

Jock then went on to say we could expect to get £25 each in cash, which was more than double what I earned in a week. Needless to say we won the game, but not by seven clear goals it was actually 12-0. Who says money can't be an incentive! To be fair, we weren't thinking about the cash as we knocked the goals in, we knew we were a good side and we were having fun, just as we seemed to in most matches.

Of course while we were playing in the reserves the first team were carving out a piece of history for themselves and the club. In 1967 Celtic reached the final of the European Cup and in front of 56,000 in Lisbon they beat Inter Milan 2-1 to become the first British club to lift the trophy. It was a remarkable achievement and a wonderful occasion for the club, its fans - and me.

Although I was on provisional forms and had become part of the playing set-up at Celtic Park, I was still very much a fan as well. That's why, when the team reached the European Cup Final, I decided I wanted to be there to share in the whole experience. So I booked myself a place with the Celtic supporter's club and travelled to Portugal on a plane for the big game. I was going to pay for the trip myself but then big Stein found out and made sure I wasn't out of pocket, which was a really nice gesture.

It was a brilliant experience for me because not only was it the first time I had flown, but I also got to sit next to the great Charlie Tully on the way out. He was a Celtic legend, especially to kids of my age, and I lapped up all the stories he came out with during the course of the flight. I was lucky enough to have a great seat for the game, with all the wives and families of the players who were in the squad. The occasion was fantastic and the celebrations after the match were something I will always remember. There were also great scenes of celebration back home in Glasgow when the team returned. I was just like any other fan and took my place on the terraces of Celtic Park to see the triumphant victory parade as the players stood on the back of a lorry which had been decked out in Celtic colours. You began to realise what it meant to the fans and to the City. It was a magnificent season for Celtic because they also won the League, the Scottish FA Cup, and the League Cup.

One day soon after that epic European Cup win against Inter Milan Kenny, Louie and me along with a few more of the young lads, were up on the terraces at Celtic Park painting barriers and generally making ourselves busy. All of a sudden I heard Jock's voice booming out as he stood at the side of the pitch.

"Gory," he shouted. "Get yourself down here." At first I was a bit worried that I might have done something wrong, but as I got nearer to him I could see he had a smile on his face.

"Take this," he said holding out his hand and in it was a bundle of cash. "Share it out amongst the other lads."

Big Jock knew none of us had been involved in the game in Lisbon but at the same time he clearly didn't want us to feel as though we were missing out on all the success. It was a bonus for all of us of more than £20 which really came in handy, and just as I started to run back up the terraces to share out the money with the rest of the boys, Stein shouted to me again.

"Here Gory," he added, handing me another £20. "That's for you and Louie because you've been here the longest."

It was a lovely gesture from the big man and typical of him in many ways. He was a great believer in everyone being a real part of the club and that was his way of making sure we all felt included.

That year proved to be a memorable and exciting one for me. Of course, there was the European Cup win and the fact that Celtic seemed to mop up everything in sight on the trophy front, and it was also the year that I became a full-time professional with the club when I signed a contract in December 1967.

John Gorman

But the real highlight came in the summer when Myra walked into my life for the first time, in that little village hall that I mentioned earlier. As I've said, it didn't take long for us to start seeing each other on a regular basis and she soon began to share in all the hopes and dreams when it came to my football career. We seemed to get on ever so well and it was great for me to have someone who was so interested and supportive right from the word go.

When Celtic decided to offer professional terms it was another big step, but at the same time I was under no illusions about the task facing me if I was ever going to break into the first team. As much as I loved the fact that the club had just won the European Cup and had probably the best team in their history, I was also well aware that with so many good players around, chances were going to be limited. It was just a fact of life at the time and it was no different for any of the other lads, but we all knew we were good players and it was no disgrace to have to bide your time and continue to learn your trade in the reserves. Big Jock was a great one for involving younger players, not just in training but also by giving them a chance to taste the action with the first team on some trips.

I remember that when I'd first arrived at the club I was really in awe of all the first team players and so were the other groundstaff boys. Remember, these guys had been real heroes to us all and I will always recall the time Billy McNeill, who was my personal hero, came along to the Player of the Year award at Uphall Saints and presented me with the trophy I had won. He even sat next to me all night and chatted, which meant so much to me. So it's no surprise that as youngsters at Celtic we literally used to keep our heads bowed if we were cleaning out a dressing room and some of the first team came in. It wasn't their fault but just the way we reacted to being in the same room as our boyhood heroes. It may sound silly, but that's how much respect we had for them. When I look back now I honestly believe I got a very good grounding from my time at Celtic. I played with good players and gradually learnt my trade. It's not something that really seems to happen in the same way these days, but times change and maybe the expectation level of youngsters now is different.

There was a very good spirit within the club as a whole and when it came to the "Quality Street Kids", we really hit it off. We were all friends on and off the pitch, but within the group there was another tight little circle, which was Davie Hay, Jimmy Quinn, Geordie Connelly, David Cattenach and me. I don't know how it happened but we just seemed to click and got on ever so well. The two Davids were very good footballers who could pass well and had a lot of skill. Jimmy was a great striker and one of the quickest players I've ever seen, and then there was big Geordie. He was a marvellous player and great defender. George had the skill and calmness of Franz Beckenbauer and although he made a big name for himself with Celtic, his story as a player was a real tragedy, because just at the time when he was set to go on to even bigger and better things, he called it a day. George made the breakthrough into the first team and went on to make more than 250 appearances for Celtic and play for Scotland. But after several well publicised walk-outs he finally quit the game in 1975. Anyone who saw him play was in no doubt that he was special and it was evident from the very first day I saw him training with Celtic.

The sessions that Big Jock put on were always enjoyable and a lot of work was done with the ball at your feet. In many ways the pre-seasons were the best, because although there had to be an emphasis on getting everyone fit you also had your own ball, and did a lot of work with it. Even when we were running around the pitch we would often have the ball at our feet as we did it and then at each corner Jock, or one of the other coaching staff would be there playing little one-twos with you. We played lots of eight and five-a-side games and it was clear that in order to be part of the Celtic set-up at that time you had be someone who was comfortable with the ball, wherever you played in the team.

I've already mentioned that the reserve team was pretty good and we actually used to play practise matches against the famous "Lisbon Lions" who had won the European Cup, and also played against them in front of the supporters at Celtic Park. We certainly held our own and the whole group of players were fanatical about the game. We just loved playing, so much so that we even did it in our own time when we were away from the club. Quite often on a Saturday after a game we'd all head off to Davie Cattenach's place in Falkirk. He had quite a big house at the time and there would be maybe a dozen couples who would make the trip. First of all we'd go off to a hotel for a drink and a laugh and then back to Davie's house for some more drinks and a sing-song, but the real business of the weekend happened the next morning. That's when we'd play our five-a-side games and believe me, we'd really go for it. There was certainly no holding back, and at half-time we'd all have an egg or bacon roll and a cup of tea before going out into the garden to finish off the game. There would be people like Kenny Dalglish, Lou Macari, Vic Davidson, Danny McGrain, George Connelly, Davie Hay, Jimmy Quinn, Davie Cattenach and me all scrapping around taking the match just as seriously as any game we might play in for Celtic, and by this time some of the lads had broken into the first team or were certainly on the verge of doing so.

I also used to play football during the close-season, not just me but a whole bunch of players who were with professional clubs. We formed an unofficial 'team' which played against local sides and those games could get pretty tasty, believe me. It seems crazy now, but I suppose it's the equivalent of Premiership players today from the London area getting together to play against sides on Hackney Marshes. We did it simply because we loved the game so much and just enjoyed playing.

Although I was doing well and getting praise for my performances in the reserves I was also finding it difficult to take that next step into the first team, not because I lacked ability, it was simply because of the quality of players already in there at left-back, but I finally made the breakthrough in 1968. It came in a League Cup quarter-final second leg against Hamilton Academicals on 25 September. We had already won the first leg at home 10-0, so I suppose it was a pretty safe bet that we'd get through! Jock took the opportunity to stick me in the first team from the start and at half-time he also blooded another young player when Kenny Dalglish came on for Charlie Gallagher. We won the game 4-2 in front of just 4,000 people and I thought I played pretty well. But instead of getting the chance of another match I was back in the reserves after that, and although I was around the first team, I never actually started another match for them.

It's something which is still a source of regret to this day, because I was convinced I could have made it and played in the first team for many years had things worked out differently for me, but it just wasn't to be and I eventually found myself being transferred from my beloved Celtic, although not before I got a taste of European action and a reminder of just how pointless it was to ever try to bet against little Louie Macari.

CHAPTER 4

UNITED IN CARLISLE

The brief experience I'd had of first team football had obviously whetted my appetite for more, but I quickly found out how hard it was going to be for me. I remember soon after the game with Hamilton Lou Macari and I trained with the first team. I thought I was finally going to be on my way, but Jock came over and said that although we'd done well we weren't going to be in the side. I was absolutely gutted, and I think I actually had tears in my eyes as I left the training session, but there was a bit of a silver lining to the cloud that hung over me that day.

Jock had obviously been impressed enough to think that we might be useful to his European plans. Celtic had been drawn against the very good French side, St Etienne, in the first round of the 1968-69 season, and one day when Louie and I were in the dressing room big Jock bounced in as only he could and seemed to fill the place with his presence.

"Great news lads," he said. "St Etienne. The first leg away, I want you to be involved."

Lou and I looked at each other and we were absolutely thrilled with the news, but then Jock took the wind out of our sails with his next comment.

"The only thing is, there's just room in the squad for one of you," he added. "So I think the fair way to do things is to toss a coin and the winner comes on the trip."

That decision didn't worry Lou one little bit, he loved to have a gamble and quick as a flash told me what would happen.

"If I were you Gory I wouldn't bother, there's only one winner and that'll be me," he chuckled.

Sure enough, he was right and won the toss. I made the long journey home feeling deeply depressed at having got so close to some more first team action, only to have the prospect snatched away from me by the toss of a coin! As soon as I walked in the house my mum could tell that I was upset. I was 19-years-old and still lived at home in Winchburgh, making the journey each day to Glasgow. As I sat in the house feeling sorry for myself she suddenly shouted out to me.

"There's a big car just pulled up outside son," she said. "I think it's someone for you."

Sure enough, she was right and as soon as I looked out of the window I could see it was George Connelly, one of the few players from our group who actually owned a car. It was clear that George was bursting to tell me something and as I opened the front door to let him in I could see he had a big grin on his face.

"Gory you're going," he said. "The big man made a mistake, he needs a defender for the squad, so you're back in."

It was great news for me and the trip turned out to be a marvellous experience. I didn't actually play in the game, and was on the bench as we lost 2-0, but St Etienne were swept aside in the return leg as Celtic ran out 4-0 winners to go through on aggregate. The European adventure that season ended at the quarter-final stage against AC Milan and I never got another real taste of first team action.

It was pretty much the same the following season for me and I had to just get on with playing regularly for the reserves. It wasn't quite the same for Geordie Connelly. He was an exceptional talent and had broken into the first team, carving himself a place in Celtic history in the 1969 Scottish Cup Final when we beat Rangers 4-0. He did it with a cheeky goal that saw him dispossess John Greig of Rangers, before sending the keeper, Norrie Martin, the wrong way and running the ball into an empty net. That night we all went back to George's place in Kincardine and had a great party. All the "Quality Street Kids" were there. It was as if we'd played in the game ourselves, because we were all so proud of what he'd done and pleased for him. That was the great thing about us. Of course we all wanted to play in the first team, but there was never a hint of jealousy when someone like George made the breakthrough, we were just genuinely happy for him.

Jock knew he was dealing with someone who was pure class when it came to Geordie and also that he could play him at the back or in a midfield role. That was the position he had when he played a crucial part in the first leg of a European Cup semi-final encounter with Leeds United in 1970 scoring the only goal of the game at Elland Road with a shot that took a deflection off of Paul Madeley's shin before going past keeper Gary Sprake. I was there too, not as part of the team but with Kenny Dalglish, David Cattenach and his best mate and business partner, Alex Smith, who drove us down to Leeds from Glasgow. Alex was a great lad and we all used to socialise together, he knew Leeds skipper Billy Bremner and had arranged for us to stay at his house, but when we got there it was all locked up and we ended up breaking in through a window.

After the game all of us went back to Billy's and it was great for me to be there celebrating a Celtic win and at the same time rubbing shoulders and talking football with some of the great players Leeds had at the time. People like Bremner, Jack Charlton, and Eddie Gray. They had a fantastic team and that's what made the tie so special, it was the English champions against the Scottish champions in what was billed as the "Battle of Britain." The second leg was played at Hampden Park in front of 134,000 people with Celtic finishing off the job by recording a 2-1 win and booking a place in the Milan final against Feyenoord. Mind you, after that first leg win it was back to reality with a bump for Kenny and me because the next night we were on duty for the reserves!

I did go to the final as part of the official party, but never played any part in the squad that night. The game finished in a 2-1 defeat for Celtic after extra-time, which was a big disappointment, especially as we went into the match as favourites. But it was a great experience for me and we stayed in a lovely hotel near Lake Como. I also managed to steer clear of any trouble, unlike the time a few years earlier when I had gone to Italy as part of a Celtic youth team and got in trouble for having a joy ride on a few pushbikes we'd found parked in a street. We were told in no uncertain terms never to bring the name of Celtic Football Club into disrepute, and the message certainly stuck with all of us.

If 1967 was a memorable year for the reasons I have already explained,

John Gorman

then 1970 could certainly be put into that category as well, because apart from Celtic reaching another European Cup Final, it was also the year I got married, bought a house, and then found myself catapulted into a new life in England with Carlisle United.

We were married on 27 June and it was one of the happiest days of my life. Myra and I were very much in love and despite the fact that I had not made a real breakthrough into the Celtic first team, I still felt I had a big future at the club and there was an awful lot for the two of us to look forward to. I had my Celtic mates at the wedding and the great thing was that all the couples in our group of friends got on well together and would often go out socially. The day went off without a hitch, which was more than could be said for my stag night.

As it was the summer I was playing football off-season in the team I described earlier, which was made up of professional players from quite a few clubs, who just wanted to get together for a kick about against local sides, just for the fun of it and the love of football. On the evening of my stag night it was decided we'd literally kick-off proceedings with a game of football, before moving on for a few drinks and a laugh. The trouble was that our game got so heated the referee had to abandon the match. The two sides were kicking lumps out of each other and it got pretty physical, happily there were no broken legs and nobody got badly injured. With pre-season training just a matter of weeks away can you imagine Big Jock's reaction if he'd found out why some of his squad were missing and how they had picked up their injuries?

After a lovely honeymoon in Majorca we returned to set up home in what was to be the first of many houses we would have in the years to come. It was a great time for both of us and Myra had been the driving force behind us deciding to actually buy our own home. I remember Jock being amazed that we would want to buy something, which might seem a bit strange. It was actually Myra's father, Lewis, who suggested it would be a good idea and I think he saw it as a sound investment for the both of us as we started our married life. Setting up home and getting everything together is always exciting and when we bought our house we thought we'd probably be spending a few years in it before maybe looking to move on. Little did we know when we returned from honeymoon that we'd only be in the place for a matter of months before having to move south to England.

In those days if your club decided you were on your way to another team, there was very little a player could do about it. There were no agents acting on your behalf and your future was really in the hands of the manager. If he wanted you on your way, it was time to start saying your goodbyes. End of story. That was pretty much the way it was with me when Big Jock decided I was surplus to requirements and did a deal to sell to me to Carlisle United. It came completely out of the blue and when he pulled me to one side and told me what was going to happen, I was totally shocked. We were doing a little warm-up run around the track, and when he called me I thought he was going to say that I was in the first team, but I couldn't have been more wrong. I'd always had a lot of praise for my performances in the reserves and still believed I could go on and make a name for myself in a Celtic shirt. I was Celtic mad and certainly didn't want to leave the club. I wanted to stay and was gutted when Jock broke the news. If I'm honest, I've always felt I was cheated out of having a career with Celtic. I didn't just leave, I was pushed.

I actually asked Stein why he was letting me go and he basically said that he was spoilt for choice in my left-back position. He said he could put Jim Brogan in there, or David Hay and of course he also had European Cup

John Gorman

winner Tommy Gemmell. In fact, what happened after I left was that Tommy had an injury and they ended up playing centre-forward, Jimmy Quinn, at left-back.

I'll be honest and say that leaving Celtic is something that I will always be a bit angry and bitter about. To leave the club that I loved with such a passion was a terrible blow to me, but it soon became clear that I had no other option and I didn't really have a say in the matter.

Big Jock and the Carlisle manager, Bob Stokoe, were mates and I later found out that my move apparently came about because Carlisle had another former Celtic player, Willie O'Neill, who had suffered a really bad Achilles injury which had put him out of action. It seems that Bob then went back to Stein and basically asked if he had another good young full-back who might fit the bill. I think Jock did it as a favour. Stokoe probably knew of me anyway, because in those days a lot of English managers and coaches would cross the border to check out the playing talent in Scotland, and I think Dick Young, who was the Carlisle coach, saw me playing for the reserves. I'd also played against the Carlisle first team in that friendly game which the Celtic reserve side won.

As soon as it was decided I would be on my way, things began to move fast. Jock drove me down the A74 to a little restaurant outside Carlisle to meet Stokoe and sort out the deal. In actual fact, I never saw the inside of the place because all the talking was done in the car park. Bob said how keen he was to sign me and told me what the wages would be. They were a big improvement on what I'd been paid at Celtic, but I would happily have sacrificed the extra cash for the chance to stay on at Celtic Park. It soon became clear there was no chance of that happening and I resigned myself to the fact that I would be moving on.

GORY TALES

Although I had no real say in whether Celtic wanted me or not, and the deal with Carlisle had already been set up, I still wanted to make sure that I didn't sell myself short. The fee was going to be £12,500 and I certainly hadn't wanted to be transferred. I asked Jock how much I would be getting out of it all as my signing-on fee and was told it would be something like £500, but I said that wasn't enough. I'd just got married, we had a new house and now I was going to be expected to just move and start all over again. Jock clearly wanted me to go, so much so that he then said he'd give me £1,500 to make sure it all went through smoothly. That was a huge sum of money back then, especially for a 21-year-old lad who had just got married. I agreed everything before going back home to tell Myra and the rest of my family that I was officially on my way.

Things happened pretty quickly after that and I suppose I just got swept along with everything. Poor Myra was left in Scotland as I headed down to Carlisle to begin a new stage in my career. I wasn't sure what was going to happen if I'm honest, but I did have faith in my own ability and I knew that Bob Stokoe thought I was a good young player. I went down to watch Carlisle in a midweek game against Manchester City in the League Cup, just to get a look at my new team mates and thought they seemed a very good side, making me wonder if I was going to struggle to get a place. After all the frustration of not being able to make a real breakthrough at Celtic, I certainly didn't want a repeat performance.

As things turned out I actually had to wait about three months before I finally did get into the side. I began to wonder if I'd made a big mistake, especially on my first full day with the club. I got the train down from Edinburgh to Carlisle and was met by chief scout Hughie Neil. He was a lovely guy and took me home to his house where his wife cooked me a beautiful steak. So far so good I thought, but then things started to change.

"Come on John," Hughie said to me after I'd eaten. "I've got you sorted out to play in a match."

I assumed he meant a practise game or a reserve match, but Hughie had other ideas.

"We're off to play down at the Sheep Mount," he added.

When we got there I couldn't believe my eyes. It was basically a local park with various pitches on it and I was in a team that wasn't even part of Carlisle United. It turned out that because the club never actually ran a reserve side and had a small squad of players, they used these games to give some of the lads match practise. They could play a couple of players in what was basically a local side. I was back to playing parks football. I wondered what the hell I'd let myself in for. I may not have been a regular in the first team at Celtic, but I was on the fringes, and part of one of the biggest clubs in Europe. In a matter of days I'd gone from that to playing on a park pitch. It was unbelievable!

So there I was, with a new club and no real prospect of going into the first team. I just had to put up with the situation knowing that sooner or later I would get my chance and when it came I fully intended to grab it with both hands. That chance eventually came along in a match against Bristol City and, as often happens, it was at the expense of an injured player. Derek Hemstead was the unlucky guy and I went on for about five minutes of the game. In the week after the match Bob Stokoe called me in and said he was going to play me in the next game, which was against Portsmouth. He even gave me the choice of playing at left or right back. I told him I preferred to play on the left and sure enough, that was where I made my first start for the club. I had a really good game, getting forward and crossing the ball for fun, we chalked up a win and I never really looked back. Pretty soon I was a permanent fixture in the Carlisle team and began to settle into my new life.

Myra moved down to join me and we rented a house from the club for the equivalent of about £2.50 per week. Before that I had stayed with Willie O'Neill. Carlisle owned several houses and it meant that when they signed players they could have somewhere to live straight away which worked well, especially if the player was married and maybe had a young family. It also meant I lived near several of the other lads and we all got on well socially and I'm sure it helped Myra to settle in. When I had broken the shock news about us having to move she didn't complain, but instead just got on with making sure everything went as smoothly as possible. I wasn't earning a fortune, but the £35 a week I was getting at Carlisle was almost double what I'd been on at Celtic, making things better for us financially. It was a big adventure for both of us, we were still only kids really and in a very short time we'd made good friends and settled into our new environment.

I'd realised quickly that there were some good players at the club, and during my time at Carlisle I was lucky enough to play with great lads. People like Chris Balderstone, Stan Bowles, Frank Clarke, Bill Green, Stan Ternent, Allan Ross, Joe Laidlaw, Graham Winstanley, Hugh McIlmoyle, Dennis Martin, Peter Carr and Les O'Neill, who became a great friend of mine and still is to this day. I was also lucky enough to be part of a magical season in the club's history, when against all the odds we reached the heights of English football's top division.

The man who signed me, Bob Stokoe, didn't hang around too long after I arrived, leaving to take over at Blackpool, and in his place Carlisle appointed Ian Macfarlane. In my first full season with the club Carlisle finished in a very respectable fourth position in the old Second Division, the equivalent to the

John Gorman

Championship these days. It gave everyone hope that there was real promise for the future, but unfortunately it proved to be a bit of a false dawn because in the season that followed we ended up in 10th place. On a personal note, the season was a real triumph for me, because I had really managed to establish myself in the team and was voted Carlisle's first ever Player of the Year. I also got to captain the side in a friendly match against my old club Celtic, at Brunton Park. I played in midfield that night marking my old mate Kenny Dalglish, and just as an added bonus I managed to score and we won the game.

There was another managerial change during the summer of 1972, when Alan Ashman, who had been in charge for four years before leaving in 1967, returned to the club. But before he'd actually taken over we'd all had a very short summer break due to the fact that we were entered for the Anglo-Italian tournament, played in the first two weeks of June. It meant that after our last game of the season at Queens Park Rangers, we were back at Brunton Park a couple of weeks later to prepare for our "Italian Job."

We flew out to play AS Roma and Catanzaro with Dick Young, who was our coach, in charge for the tournament. Dick was a great trainer, who was known as "The Silver Fox" he had grey hair and had been around in the game for a long time. To this day I consider him one of the best coaches I've ever worked with in football. Even now a lot of his coaching drills stand the test of time, and I've certainly leaned on some of his methods over the years.

Our first game against Roma was played in the Olympic Stadium, although it felt a bit like the Coliseum because the crowd were right on our backs, throwing coins whenever they could and really having a go. But it didn't stop us causing a real upset by beating the Italians 3-2 on their own turf. And I'll always remember Stan Bowles juggling the ball in the middle of the pitch, showing Roma just what a good player he was. Poor Stan got a shock soon after we arrived in Italy and checked into our hotel. Just like a bunch of excited schoolboys we got changed and went straight down to the pool, determined to make the most of our European excursion. Stan was the first in the pool, and produced a brilliantly executed dive which looked superb from our sun beds as we as looked on. Unfortunately he emerged from the water with blood pouring from his nose, having dived in the shallow end by mistake!

Stan scored the only goal of the game as we beat Catanzaro in our second game three days later, but one of the real highlights for me was getting to see the Pope. There were about three or four of us in the squad who were Catholics and I suggested we went off to try and get a glimpse of the Pope. In the end we managed to go one better and were given special passes which allowed us into a part of the Vatican where we were no more than an arm's length away from him. It was a great experience for me and just added to the enjoyment of the whole trip.

Back at Brunton Park a crowd of 12,000 turned out to see us play the return leg against Roma. I was presented with the Player of the Year trophy on the pitch before the game and we drew the match 3-3 after leading 3-1 at one stage. A few days later we beat Catanzaro 4-1, but despite the good performances, it was Blackpool and not us who finished top of the English section. Roma somehow managed to finish top of the Italian teams and later defeated Blackpool 3-0 at the Olympic Stadium in the tournament final.

Playing first team football on a regular basis was good for me and having won the Player of the Year trophy, it was clear that other people appreciated what I was doing on the pitch as well. During my time at the club I collected three of the trophies, and the great thing was that a couple of them came with an added bonus. One award brought Myra and me a free holiday in Majorca, and another allowed us to have free meat for a year! Not bad when you consider that the salaries on offer for players at that level were considerably less than they get now in the Championship.

Although my money was a big improvement on what I'd been getting at Celtic, it was by no means a fortune and because of that I used to supplement my wages in the summer by doing other jobs. One summer Myra got a job doing some office work for a local bakery, and I earned a bit extra driving one of their vans. I actually nearly crashed once because I was so tired that I fell asleep at the wheel. I also had a summer job with the building firm Barrett Homes, which was more of a meet-and-greet affair in one of the show houses they were building at the time in Carlisle. Doing another job out of season was something a lot of the players did. I know it seems hard to imagine today, but that's the way it was. Chris Balderstone also had another "job" out of season, but his was a bit better than mine. He played County cricket and got into hot water in the summer of 1973 for not returning to Carlisle on time and instead continuing to play for Leicestershire, earning him a club suspension.

The season before had been a bit of a disappointment on the football front for all of us, and we only managed to finish in 18th place. With form like that we weren't exactly the bookies favourites to make an impact in the promotion race as the 1973-74 season began. To be honest, I wasn't too confident myself after our second game of the season when we went down 6-1 at Luton. In fact we only managed one win in our first six league matches, but some of the other lads had more faith than me and I remember Chris being very positive about our chances. He knew we had a good team and some very good players, even if we did have a small squad.

GORY TALES

We began to turn things around a bit after those first half dozen games when we found ourselves second from bottom. It all started to come together and as well as climbing the table we also had a couple of good FA Cup results that season, beating the holders Sunderland away after a replay and then drawing against mighty Liverpool at Anfield in the fourth round before losing at Brunton Park. But it was the final few weeks of the season that provided the real excitement for everyone at the club.

We played our last home game of the season against Aston Villa and the 2-0 win we got with goals from Joe Laidlaw and Frank Clarke was enough to take us into third place. It was the first time that season we'd actually managed to get into the promotion places and at the end of the match big Bill Green, who was our skipper but was injured and hadn't played in the game, came running on and lifted me up.

"We're promoted, we're promoted," he kept screaming, but it was all a false alarm because we were relying on other results. Blackpool had needed to win to keep their hopes alive, but had lost at Sunderland, while Orient drew at Cardiff meaning they were two points behind us but with a game in hand. They'd been due to play at home against Villa earlier in the season, but the fixture had been postponed and re-arranged as the Londoner's last game of the season. It meant Orient would have to beat Villa six days later in order to claim the last promotion place. So all we could do was sit it out and hope. A couple of the boys actually went down to London on the Friday to watch the game and sat there nervously counting down the minutes before finally seeing Villa hold the home side to a draw. That was it. We were up. Unbelievably little old Carlisle United were going to be rubbing shoulders with the big boys of English football.

Not surprisingly the town went mad. Everyone seemed to be celebrating and the fans turned out to see us at a civic reception. Mind you, a lot of them missed out because our bus driver went the wrong way. There we all were expecting to see the usual streets lined with fans, but we hardly saw anyone. We were all joking that maybe the supporters didn't think much of us after all when we found out that the driver was taking the shortest route and was a bit lost, we ended up going into the back entrance at the Civic Centre.

The excitement lasted right through the summer and when the season began, nobody could have written the script for what happened in the first three games, which saw us at the top of the First Division looking down on the rest of football's elite.

Our first match of the season was away to Chelsea and I was up against my old pal Davie Hay who had joined the Stamford Bridge club from Celtic. As a nice gesture their players applauded us onto the pitch at the start, but I'm not sure too many of them would have felt as friendly at the end of the game because we beat them 2-0 with goals from Bill Green in the first couple of minutes, and another by Les O'Neill 15 minutes from time. Les got both goals in our 2-0 win at Middlesbrough in our next game and then a Chris Balderstone penalty gave us a 1-0 win against Tottenham in our first ever home match in the top flight. Three games, three wins and we were top of the League. It was a fantastic feeling even if the season was only a week old and everyone connected with the club enjoyed making the most of it. The great thing was that we hadn't got the three wins by luck, we had played good football and competed in each of the games. I missed the Tottenham match but remember how proud I was of the lads beating such a famous team like Spurs, little knowing that I would go on to have such strong connections with the White Hart Lane club later in my career.

Unfortunately, the fairytale didn't last for too much longer and after that win against Tottenham we only managed to record two more victories in our next 17 matches. By the time we lost 3-1 at Ipswich at the end of November on a very heavy pitch we were one off the bottom of the table. It was in that game that I suddenly felt a really acute pain in my stomach, but like most players I just wanted to play and instead of coming off I carried on and probably made the whole thing a lot worse.

By the time the next game came around I was in real agony but I wanted to play. It was at home against Arsenal and nobody gave us a chance because of our poor form, but I had some treatment and got on with it. We managed to upset the odds once more winning 2-1 and I had a great game, possibly one of my best ever. I got great write-ups in the papers with some people comparing me to the Leeds and England full-back, Terry Cooper. Our next match was also at home, against Chelsea, and David Hay told me that they were intending to play winger Charlie Cooke to try and make sure I didn't get forward and cause the trouble I had against Arsenal.

Once again I was in absolute agony in the week leading up to the game and it was decided the best thing I could do was rest. On the eve of the match I went to see a specialist, who first froze an area of my groin, and then gave me a second injection to help deaden the pain and enable me to play the next day. My father and brother, together with Myra's dad all used to come down on the train from Edinburgh to watch the home games at Carlisle because it wasn't too far to travel. When my brother saw me on the evening before the Chelsea match he couldn't believe it. I'd just got back from having my injections and was slumped in a chair. I was so sore that he had to help me get out of it.

"There's no way you can play tomorrow," he told me.

I knew it must have looked bad, but by the time the game came around I was fine and played in the match, which we lost 2-1. After that the regular weekly routine stayed pretty much the same. Most of the time it was rest and then maybe a light training session before going off to get my injections. It all became very matter-of-fact for me, although there was one visit which I will never forget. It was all going well with the doctor chatting away in his usual fashion as he applied the freezing solution with his needle, when I suddenly felt an excruciating pain in a very sensitive part of my body.

"Oh dear!" said the specialist. "The needle's hit your testicle."

He didn't have to tell me. I was already well aware that he'd stuck it where he shouldn't have. Just as he spoke to me the nurse who was assisting him looked across at the needle sticking out of a very private part of my body and promptly fainted. The specialist immediately left me clutching at the syringe, and went and comforted her!

Luckily that little episode was never repeated but I still had to keep up the treatment. I missed some games around the Christmas period and from February until the end of the season I was in and out of the side because of the injury. I was around to play in a home FA Cup quarter-final tie with Fulham, when we played really well but missed out on a chance to get into the semi-final, losing to the only goal of the game scored by Les Barrett.

I missed out on the last two games of the season but by that time it was all over for us and we finished bottom of the league. It had been a great adventure for everyone connected with the club. I'd tasted football in the top division and knew I wanted more. I loved Carlisle, the club and its fans, but at the same time I realised I had to get away.

CHAPTER 5

EARNING MY SPURS

Carlisle still holds very happy memories for me to this day, and not just on the playing front. Both of my children, Amanda and Nick, were born there and we made some great friends while I was at the club.

Getting into the First Division was a magnificent achievement for Carlisle when you think of the small crowds and limited resources they had. Alan Ashman managed to fashion a very good footballing side, who were well coached by Dick Young, but the fact was that the season we had in the top division was never likely to be repeated. I think all the players realised that and I wasn't the only one who, having had a taste of the First Division, wanted to get back there. If it wasn't going to be with Carlisle then it had to be with another club.

I made it clear that I wanted to get away and refused to sign a new contract. I knew other clubs had taken note of my performances and I also knew that the club had turned down a bid of more than £100,000 from Stoke while we were in the First Division. It happened in February 1975 when the Stoke full-back, Mike Pejic, broke his leg in a match against Wolves. Alan Ashman actually called me in and said he'd had the offer but that the Stoke manager, Tony Waddington, was a good friend of his and it wouldn't have been fair to him letting me go because at the time I'd had the stomach injury. I was absolutely livid. Stoke were a very decent side with people like Peter Shilton, Alan Hudson and Geoff Hurst at the club. In the season we got relegated they finished fifth and would clearly have been a step up for me, but Ashman wouldn't have it. I was so angry after he told me that I drove away from the ground without looking properly and had a crash.

I'd also seen stories in the newspapers speculating on whether I would be moving from Carlisle. On one occasion I was sitting up in bed on the morning of a match reading a paper and there was a story in it with quotes from Gordon Jago, the former Queens Park Rangers manager, saying that one of the reasons he had left the club was because he didn't have the sort of funds to go out and buy me for £100,000. I hadn't even been aware he was interested because Carlisle never said anything.

I knew the only way to get a transfer in that season after our relegation was to make sure I maintained a decent level of performance. I suppose I was a wee bit big-headed in a way, but I was 26-years-old, with a wife, a house and two young kids. A footballer's life is a relatively short one and I wanted to make the most of mine. In the season after we went down I was an ever-present and ended up getting my third Player of the Year trophy. I think some of the fans didn't like the fact that I made no secret of my desire to get away, but it still showed that I was getting on with my job and that the supporters appreciated it. It didn't help that people like Bill Green, who went to West Ham, and Ray Train who was transferred to Sunderland, managed to get away. I began to feel jealous and thought it was never going to happen for me.

Alan Ashman had resigned from the club after a few months of the season following our relegation, and Dick Young took over as caretaker manager before being given the job on a permanent basis, but it wasn't a good season for us and we only managed to make sure we stayed up on the last day of the campaign.

Dick remained as manager at the start of the next season and things didn't improve too much on the playing front. We only got three wins from our first dozen league games and it was pretty evident that although Dick was a tremendous coach, he wasn't really enjoying being a manager. He just didn't seem cut out for it, not that the lack of success on the pitch was down to him, there had been a bit of a change around in personnel and I don't think that helped but the bottom line was that we just weren't consistent enough.

At the beginning of November 1976 we played a home game against Bolton and lost 1-0. I was marking Willie Morgan the former Scotland and Manchester United winger, and I had an absolute stinker. I came home from that match and told Myra that after a performance like that nobody was going to be interested in me. I still hadn't signed a new contract with Carlisle, which in those days meant that if there was any transfer it would have to be settled by a tribunal, and I could suddenly see my worth in the market plunging because of the way I'd played.

A couple of days later I went into training and there were loads of cars parked outside the ground. I wondered what was up, because usually that sort of activity signalled a coming or going on the playing front. I found out

John Gorman

that the reason for all the interest was Dick, he'd quit as manager and Bobby Moncur the former Newcastle captain and Scottish international was going to take over.

As I've said, both Amanda and Nick were born in Carlisle. Amanda came along in July 1973 and I was there to witness the birth, but when Nick arrived in August 1976 I was on a pre-season tour with the team and missed his arrival. I got a phone call from Myra instead to tell me I had a little son, and it was a fantastic moment, although he's never let me forget that I wasn't around for him but was for his sister!

That day after all the fuss about Bobby Moncur becoming the new manager, Myra and I decided to take little Amanda for a walk along with her baby brother in his pushchair. Just as we were getting towards our house I heard the phone ringing and for some reason decided to sprint home and answer it. I picked it up trying to catch my breath and at the same time heard the voice of Dick Young on the other end of the line.

"John, it's Dick," he said. "Tottenham Hotspur."

"Yeah," I replied. "What about them?"

"They want to sign you, the deal's been done," he added in a very matter-of-fact way.

By this time Myra had walked into the house with the children and could see I was excited, but at the same time I was deliberately playing the whole thing down as I spoke to Dick.

"Oh, do they Dick?" I asked him trying to sound as cool as I could.

"Well you don't sound very excited about it," he said clearly becoming exasperated by my attitude. "It's bloody Tottenham Hotspur John. Now get down to the ground, collect your boots and you're booked on the London train this evening. Their manager will meet you with his chairman."

GORY TALES

I had already spoken to the Professional Footballer's Association, who were the player's union, because of my situation. Having refused to sign a contract they were helping to monitor things and kept me informed of any interest from other clubs. I knew that Manchester City had been interested, but when I heard that Tottenham were after me that was it. They were a massive club with a great tradition and a history of winning trophies, I didn't even check to see what their league position was, if I had I'd have noticed that it mirrored Carlisle's – both clubs were 20th in their respective leagues, but the big difference was that Spurs were in the First Division which was where I wanted to play my football.

Although I had tried to be as calm as possible on the phone to Dick, I was jumping around like a kid when I hung up and told Myra. We didn't waste any time at all and after throwing a few things into a suitcase for me she drove to the ground so that I could get my boots, just as Dick had told me to do. I suppose that once again, everything had been pretty much decided between the two clubs without me really being consulted, but unlike the move from Celtic a little over six years earlier, I didn't feel as though I was being deprived of a chance to make it at the top level. With all due respect to Carlisle, this time I was taking a step up on the football ladder, and I was determined to reach the top.

The journey to London seemed to take no time at all because I was so excited at the prospect of joining Spurs and everything had happened so quickly. Sure enough the Tottenham manager, Keith Burkinshaw and the club's chairman, Mr Wale, were there to meet me at the station and take me off to a hotel in Enfield for a medical. I have to say that it was a fairly basic medical carried out by a doctor who had probably been enjoying a glass or two of wine with his evening meal before he was called out to check me over.

John Gorman

Keith told me what wages I would be getting, which was about three times the amount I'd been earning at Carlisle, and I signed my contract. No long drawn out negotiations, no agents, and no real thought as to how the rest of the family was going to cope with the move. That was the way things were done, and I doubt that my transfer was very different to so many of the deals during the 1970's. Spurs paid £60,000 for me I signed on the Wednesday night and settled back on my hotel bed trying to get some sleep before taking part in my first training session the next morning.

I soon discovered that Tottenham was a completely different world to the club I had come from. The good thing was that it felt like a very friendly place from the first day and that helped me to settle in. The first person I met when I turned up at the club's training ground in Cheshunt, was a tall 19-year-old kid who had already earned a reputation for himself as midfield player with exceptional ability. His name was Glenn Hoddle and for some reason we seemed to hit it off straight away, even though I was eight years older than him. The rest of the lads all introduced themselves and it was then that it hit me just how different things were going to be.

Although Spurs weren't doing too well at the time they still had some very big names at the club, and the squad was sprinkled with international players. On that first morning at Cheshunt we had a full-scale 11-a-side practise match and I was up against the Northern Ireland international winger Noel Brotherston. I pretty soon realised how different it was all going to be, because he was a really good little player and I had to work hard and concentrate for the whole session.

I was determined to make sure I did myself justice and even refused the offer of a night out with the other lads that day, because I wanted to prepare for the game on the Saturday, hoping Keith Burkinshaw would pick me for my Tottenham debut in the home match against Bristol City. In fact, in the three days I spent in the hotel after signing, I lost 9lbs in weight. I never ate things like desserts and certainly didn't have any alcohol, I simply wanted to be the best prepared I could for the big day. Mind you, although I found out on the Friday that I would be in the team, I nearly didn't make it at all thanks to the training routine Tottenham had at the time. Every Friday they trained in an indoor gym at the ground and played a five-a-side game, which sounds great, but I wasn't prepared for how ferocious it was. Tackles flew in from all over the place and it was something I'd never experienced at Carlisle. I remember on that first Friday getting whacked from behind by defender Terry Naylor and having my face pushed right up against the wall of the gym.

"Welcome to Tottenham!" said Terry, who was a lovely bloke but as hard as they come on the pitch.

My debut wasn't exactly one to remember as City beat us 1-0 keeping Tottenham just a couple of places off the bottom of the table. It wasn't the sort of thing expected at a club like Spurs, and I realised the kind of support they had that day against Bristol because even with results going badly almost 29,000 people turned up.

Although my debut had ended in a defeat I was still thrilled to be at Tottenham and playing in the First Division once again. I continued to stay in the hotel for a while, but then the club said I would have to find some digs to stay in. I may have been playing in the top flight of English football with one of the biggest clubs in the country, but they weren't prepared to pay for me to stay in a hotel for longer than I had to. It's often very different these days, with players being given much more time before having to find their own accommodation. As it happened a friend of mine called Tony Donaghue, who came from Winchburgh, lived in Wood Green, which was very near the Spurs ground. He rented a room at his cousin's house and because Tony was going to be working abroad for a while he suggested I take his place. It was perfect for me and I became friends with his cousin Tony Bann, his wife Ann and their children. It was a great arrangement but at the same time I was aware Myra and the children were still in Carlisle and we needed to find a house so that we could all be together as a family.

Myra had been left to do everything in Carlisle as she tried to sell our house, while at the same time cope with a young daughter and a baby son. She did manage to come down for some visits while I was still in digs and I also arranged for her to stay for the Christmas period that year. We rented a house in Enfield, which wasn't exactly in great condition, and then to top it all, I wasn't really around too much because of playing matches over the busy holiday period. The nice thing was that my Spurs and Northern Ireland team mate, Gerry Armstrong and his wife, were around to spend some time with Myra, but it was a miserable experience for her just the same. Typically, she didn't complain, but instead told me to get on with playing my football and that we'd find a house to buy as soon as we sold our place in Carlisle.

Things weren't really improving on the pitch with the team still hovering around the relegation zone and people starting to talk about the unthinkable – Tottenham going down to the Second Division.

At least I'd managed to hit some consistently good form and had become a first team regular, but at the beginning of March 1977 we went into a league game at Norwich having hit rock bottom. We'd lost four games on the spin and were looking up at the rest of the division, it was a pretty desperate state of affairs, but we went to Carrow Road and got a vital 3-1 win. Then in our next match at home to eventual champions Liverpool we recorded a superb 1-0 victory with a goal from Ralphie Coates. It should have stayed in my memory as one of the happiest nights of my career, but instead it proved to be the beginning of an injury nightmare that would eventually lead to the end of my time with Tottenham.

I went into a block tackle with Liverpool's Jimmy Case and felt a terrible pain in my left knee. I knew it was bad but didn't come to realise just how bad until some time later. It was the start of one of the worst phases in my footballing life. I've read over the years that Jimmy ruined my career, but that is absolute rubbish. Jimmy had a reputation as a hard man in Liverpool's midfield, but there was certainly nothing dirty about the tackle. It was simply one of those things and probably owed more to the fact that my own leg was in a certain position when the impact was made.

I actually tried to get fit for the next game which was at home to West Bromwich Albion, but it was no use, and it became clear that there was a real problem with the knee. The Spurs physiotherapist at the time was Mike Varney, and he arranged for me to have remedial treatment at a place in Camden, North London, where they really worked you each day with just a break for lunch.

Towards the end of the season I managed to get something like match fit and played with the reserves, hoping that I would be ready to return to first team action the following season. By this time I knew if that were to happen I would be back in the Second Division, because the unthinkable had happened. Tottenham had finished bottom of the league and been relegated.

I was fit enough to do pre-season training and as part of the build-up to the big kick-off we went on tour to Sweden. In a practise match against a local side I went into a tackle and suddenly felt the same sort of pain I'd experienced against Liverpool. Once again I was back on the treatment table being looked after by Mike Varney, going through all sorts of things in order to get me playing. After nine weeks of trying to get me fit, I had to go back and see the specialist, Mr English, who stuck me on a couch and let me see for myself the extent of the damage to my knee. He had a monitor nearby and it showed the scan of my knee. I had a medial ligament rupture and a cartilage which was torn to shreds. In short, my knee was a mess. It was decided I should have an operation inserting a screw into the knee, although it was actually more like a bolt. I was also warned by Mike that my career was in jeopardy, but I tried to shrug off the suggestion, telling him that I'd be alright and would get through it. I was determined to get fit and play again, but little did I realise at the time that I would miss a whole season as I tried to recover and regain full fitness. I'd played just 16 first team games for Spurs and it looked as though my career with them could be over before it had really started.

Any footballer who has experienced having a long-term injury will tell you just how frustrating it can be and how isolated you feel at times. Tottenham had a smashing bunch of lads playing for them at that time and we all got on really well, but while they were going off to train and play in matches, I was having to undergo remedial treatment at places like Hedley Court in Surrey, while training largely on my own and working with Mike.

By this time we'd bought a house in Nazeing, Essex, and were more settled as a family, but I obviously wanted to be playing. For the first time in my life I wasn't able to do the simple thing that had been so important to me for as long as I could remember – kick a football. The good thing was that although it was going slowly, I was being assured that progress was being made. I also had the comfort of my art work to fall back on as well.

I might have been out of the team, but I still featured in the Tottenham programme when there was a home game. Not on the playing sheet, but as the resident cartoonist. I began drawing little caricatures of all the players and each home game they would reprint one in the programme. They were quite popular and I think I soon became better known for my drawing than my football with some fans. Some had seen my art, but not seen me kick a ball in anger. The cartoons became so popular that I decided to do a calendar with a player on the page of each month, including me with a screw sticking out of my knee! I enjoyed doing it and it also made a few extra bob, because Glenn, who had become a good friend in the short time I'd been at the club, decided he would give me a helping hand. He used to drive me around to places like pubs and shops, flogging the calendars with me.

The team did well in the Second Division and were never out of the top three. At one stage it looked as though they could return to the top division by becoming champions, but in the end it was a nail-biting finish with a goalless draw at Southampton securing third place and promotion ahead of Brighton. Fellow Scot, John Duncan, who had missed much of the previous season with a back injury, returned to the side and notched 16 league goals, while Glenn played a major role by hitting a dozen from midfield. Striker Colin Lee joined the club from Torquay and scored 11 goals as did Peter Taylor, while Chris Jones got eight. The point was that the side were really good going forward and scored 73 goals that season. The whole thing really whetted my appetite and I was determined to get myself fit and ready to come back, I'd had enough of watching from the sidelines and was desperate to play first team football again in a side that looked to attack.

That summer I went to the remedial centre in Surrey and worked really hard. When I came back I felt great and I told Myra that I was going to get my first team place back. I wanted to be part of the team that started the season back with the big boys in Division One. I think she could see how desperate

John Gorman

I was to play, but at the same time she knew the game well enough to realise that I might have to face disappointment.

There was a real buzz at the club that summer and it wasn't just because of the promotion. In the early part of July, before we'd even returned to Cheshunt for pre-season training, it was announced that Keith Burkinshaw had managed to pull off two fantastic transfers by paying out around £700,000 for the services of Argentines Osvaldo Ardiles and Ricardo Villa. The two had been part of their country's victorious World Cup winning squad the previous month in Buenos Aires, with Ardiles actually playing in the team which defeated Holland 3-1 in the final. It gave everyone a tremendous lift and meant that Spurs hit the headlines on both the front and back pages of the newspapers. Tottenham were suddenly big news.

As part of the pre-season programme we were due to play games in Belgium, Holland, Scotland and Ireland. The game in Belgium was against Antwerp and it attracted a huge amount of interest because it was the match in which Ossie Ardiles and Ricky Villa made their first appearances for Tottenham.

We won 3-1 and it was clear to everyone who watched that the two of them were class players, although when we saw Ossie in training for the first time I think a lot of us thought Burky had bought the wrong player. He just kept on falling over the ball. It was amazing, he wasn't a good trainer at all, but put him in a match situation and it was a completely different scenario. He was pure magic. He seemed to glide across the field, and also had this uncanny knack of being able to come around the side of you and nick the ball out from under your feet. I think both of them were impressed with Glenn. He still wasn't 21-years-old when they arrived and was like a kid in a sweet shop when he heard the two of them had signed. Like everyone else we'd seen them on the box playing in front of huge crowds in Argentina, and to have the two boys training alongside us was a real thrill. Both of them were great guys and considering they'd just been part of a World Cup winning squad, they were very down to earth and would do anything they could to help you. I was asked by someone later in the season if I would draw them so that he could put the artwork on T-shirts and they were more than happy for me to do sketches of them. I ended up being paid £1,000 for my work, which was a hell of a lot more than I'd got for those calendars!

I got into the team for the friendly game in Dublin just before the season was due to open and was desperate to stay in the side for the first game of the campaign away to reigning champions, Nottingham Forest. I'd worked hard to get fit but although I wasn't getting any real trouble from my knee, I had picked up a strain in my left thigh. I wanted to make sure that nobody knew about it, because I realised it might mean I never got the chance to start in the first team. Keith kept asking me if I was all right and whether the knee was holding up. I told him it was fine, but never let on about the strain.

Ricky scored our goal in a 1-1 draw with Forest and the next day we witnessed the sort of impact he and Ossie already had on the club when thousands of supporters turned out at Cheshunt to see them and the rest of the squad in a special training session as part of the events for Steve Perryman's testimonial year. A few days later White Hart Lane was packed with almost 48,000 people to see our first home game with Ricky and Ossie in the side. There was a tremendous atmosphere at the ground and when we ran out onto the pitch the place erupted. The noise was deafening and the fans showered the field with ticker-tape and confetti just as they'd seen the Argentinean supporters do during the World Cup. The stage was set for a great night, but unfortunately we couldn't deliver and instead of cheering a home win, our fans had to endure a 4-1 beating.

My knee felt fine although I was conscious of the fact that I'd learnt how to adapt my play in order to compensate for the injury. If I had to take a ball that was off the ground I had to tense the muscles of my left leg before dealing with it, but it certainly wasn't stopping me from playing and I enjoyed being back in the side. I'm sure Keith was wary of using me too much and thought that the best thing might be to ease me back, but I still played in seven of the first eight league matches. We were due to play West Bromwich away and a day or two before the game Mike Varney pulled me to one side and said that he thought I needed a rest. I guess he must have said the same thing to Keith because I wasn't included for the trip to play WBA, and was left out for the five games that followed.

I was back in the side in November against Chelsea and was given another run of matches, but as the year ended my frustration began to grow, because I found myself sitting on the sidelines again, even though I felt I was playing well enough to retain my place in the side.

The weather began to play a major role during February 1979, with fixtures being disrupted and FA Cup ties being postponed because of freezing conditions. I suddenly found myself back in the team for a game at Coventry which might well have been called off because the pitch was like an ice rink. Their players were falling about all over the place, but we all kept our feet and knocked the ball around to earn a 3-1 win which owed as much to our experienced old trainer, Johnny Wallace, as it did to the players. He saw what the conditions were like before the game and immediately got to work on our boots, taking the studs off and exposing little sharpened nails. They worked a treat, giving us just the sort of grip we needed.

Like any other player I was happy if I was in the team and unhappy when

GORY TALES

I wasn't, so when Keith kept me in the side for the FA Cup fourth round home tie against Wrexham two days later, I was naturally pleased. The weather had taken its toll on games, and Wrexham got through to the fourth round after beating Stockport 6-2 in a match which was postponed no less than nine times. They were a decent side who had done well in the Second Division early on in the season, but had slipped a bit in recent weeks. We were expected to beat them comfortably, but in the end could only draw 3-3, and I didn't play well. There was snow on the pitch and my boots kept on clogging up, it was one of those games you would rather forget and a really frustrating night.

I happened to be one of the first players into our dressing room after the match and there was Burky waiting for us. Now I have a lot of respect for Keith Burkinshaw and over the years we have remained on friendly terms. He was a good manager and was very encouraging to me when I first signed for Spurs. He made me feel part of the Tottenham set-up and even sat me down one day to say how well I'd done and started picking my brains on other good players from the Second Division that I'd come across during my time with Carlisle. He was a good coach and thought a lot about the game, but on that particular night he really upset me, and I totally lost my temper. For some reason he called me a cheat, and I went mad. There was a cup of hot tea on the table and I picked it up and threw it across the room hitting Burky on the shoulder. The rest of the lads couldn't believe what I'd done. I could see they were thinking, "Are you mad Gory? You've just got back into the team and now you're throwing cups of tea at the manager!"

I got showered and changed before heading up to the players bar where some of the other lads were. They all came over to me and said I should swallow my pride and go and apologise to Keith, but I was adamant that I wasn't going to do that. I knew I'd had a bad game but I'd been trying to play well, just like the rest of the team, it was just one of those nights. We were all disappointed, but I couldn't understand why I had been singled out for criticism. The one thing I was sure about was that I'd be in trouble for my actions and any hopes of retaining my first team place probably disappeared as soon as that tea hit the manager's shoulder.

We were due to play Everton on the following Saturday and to my surprise I was in the team. It obviously showed Keith didn't hold a grudge, and he hadn't even said any more about the incident. I wanted to keep playing and knew that I needed regular match action after coming back from the injury. Steve Perryman had said to me that it might be a good idea if I approached Keith and asked if I could go on loan to America during the close-season. The North American Soccer League was really popular at that time and it was attracting some of the biggest names in the game. Some went over there on a permanent basis and others did it during our summer. It was quite a lucrative thing to do, because the American clubs were paying very good money and for someone in my position it sounded perfect. I would be able to play right through the summer and then come back fighting fit and ready for the new season. Defender Don McAllister had done it and said how much he'd enjoyed the whole experience, but when I went to have a word with Keith about the possibility of going he refused point blank. He wouldn't entertain the idea, and I think part of the reason for this was the fact that although Don had enjoyed his time in the States, he had also come back to England with an injury and no manager wants to have any of his first team squad turning up for pre-season training with injuries.

In the end the Everton game was cancelled because of poor weather, meaning that the next game was going to be the replay with Wrexham at their place, but before the team was announced Keith called me into his office. I was fully expecting him to tell me that I wasn't in the team again, but I wasn't prepared for the bombshell he hit me with.

"John, I'll be honest with you," he said sitting opposite me and at the same time looking a bit ill at ease. "I think you should quit."

"Sorry?" I replied, not quite believing what I had just heard.

"It's the injury and everything you've had to do since." added Keith. "You're never going to be the same player again."

I was devastated. One minute I was back in the team, the next minute I wasn't just out of the side, I was being told by the manager that my Tottenham career was over. I had been at White Hart Lane for a little more than two years, and during that time had really grown to love the place. I felt Tottenham were my club and although I'd had my injury problems, I knew they were behind me and believed the thing I needed most was time. But it was clear Keith wasn't prepared to give me that, he'd spoken to various people at the club and made his decision, which is exactly what a manager has to do, it was just that I felt he'd made the wrong decision.

Keith explained how he liked me and had enjoyed having me at the club as a player and then made me an offer. He was prepared to give me a youth team coaching job and at the same time I would have been entitled to more than £30,000 as part of the insurance payout for the premature end to my career. I think a lot of players would have jumped at the chance, but I was 29-years-old, and having battled back from such serious injury problems, I was determined to make the most of my playing days. I knew I still had a lot left in me, but I was realistic enough to know that I wasn't back to my best.

Long injuries take time to recover from. You can get your fitness back, but only games and lots of them, will give you back the kind of touch and match

John Gorman

fitness every player needs to perform at their best. I told Burky that there was no way I was going to quit the game. I needed more time and if Tottenham weren't going to give me that time and the chance to play I'd go somewhere else.

I realised there was no chance of me ever getting into the first team again after what Keith had told me and the next weekend I found myself being asked by our coach, Peter Shreeves to help him out and play in the reserves in a left sided midfield position.

Steve Perryman, who had first suggested me going to the States on loan, put me in touch with a couple of guys who were involved in arranging things like club tours for various teams. At the time they just happened to be talking to Gordon Jago, who was managing Tampa Bay Rowdies in Florida. They got in touch with Gordon on my behalf and asked if he would be interested in me. I knew Gordon had fancied me as a player when he was at QPR, because of the article I'd read, when he'd said he'd wanted to sign me while he was at Rangers. Ted Buxton was the Rowdies European scout and he was sent to watch me play in the reserve team. I had a good game and managed to score a goal as well. Ted contacted me and said that he'd spoken to Gordon and Tampa were interested in signing me if I was going to be given a free transfer from Spurs. I knew I could play and the thought of going to America really began to appeal to me. I went to see Keith and told him that I wanted the chance to go. Burky was very good about it and promised that he'd do everything he could to help me if I was so determined to carry on playing in the States, but he also explained that ultimately the decision wouldn't be his and the board of directors would have to make the final call. About two days later he got back to me and was as good as his word. He told me the club were prepared to release me from my contract but at the same time I had to sign an agreement basically saying that I wasn't suddenly going to pop up back in England with another club. Once that was done the path was clear for me to start a new phase in my life 4,000 miles away.

It was a huge decision for me to make, and a massive change for Myra and the children. We were going to be moving away from family and friends. Leaving the place that had become home, and I'd be lying if I said it was an easy decision, but at the same time I knew I couldn't hang around. Tampa wanted me over there for their pre-season training in April, which meant I would have to travel on my own leaving Myra to tidy up all the pieces of our life in England.

I had played exactly 32 first team league and cup matches for Tottenham. If I could have stayed clear of injury who knows how things might have worked out for me at the club?

John Gorman

CHAPTER 6

RE-BORN IN
THE USA

If I'm asked now whether I feel bitter about the way my playing days ended at
Spurs, I suppose my answer would be no, but I do feel a sense of injustice.

All I wanted was time, and I wasn't allowed to have that. From Keith
Burkinshaw's point of view I suppose he had to look at the situation and make
a decision. He probably genuinely believed I would never be the same player
I had been, but I still think that if he'd agreed to maybe loan me out for a
month or two and allow me to play regular first team football, I could have
come back and been good enough to have earned my place back. It's all a
long time ago now and having been a manager myself, I realise that you can't
keep everyone happy, and that decisions on players fitness and ability may

upset them. It's part of the game, but back in the spring of 1979 I couldn't help feeling a little cheated.

The good thing was that I had managed to sort out my move to America and the excitement of going to play in the States began to occupy my thoughts, meaning that I never really had time to sit and brood or become bitter about what had happened. One of the things I had to have sorted out before I could actually sign for the Rowdies was a medical. Not surprisingly I was a little bit anxious, my knee felt fine but at the same time I knew I'd had some major surgery and wasn't sure the specialist would give me the all-clear. Ted Buxton arranged the medical and my heart sank when the guy came into the room looking worried having given me an extensive examination.

"Is there a problem with my knee?" I asked expecting to have to convince him just how well it had felt since all of the surgery.

"No problem at all with your knee Mr Gorman," he told me. "But we're slightly concerned with your heart."

You can just imagine how I felt. I'd gone through all those months of agony and frustration because of injury, and now I was being told I had a dicky heart. As things turned out I had nothing to worry about. The "problem" they had detected was an extremely slow heart beat but it was something I'd always had, and my son Nick has inherited it from me as well. I was told what I already knew, that I was as fit as a fiddle and now had the green light to sign for the Rowdies.

I had a great night out with all the Tottenham lads before I left for Tampa and although it was sad for me in many ways, it was also great to have a laugh and joke with them all. I'd made particular friends with people like Jimmy Holmes, an Irish defender with a great sense of humour, big striker Ian

John Gorman

Moores and Gerry Armstrong, but perhaps the player who'd become my biggest mate at the club was Glenn Hoddle. I don't know why that happened but I do know we seemed to be on the same wavelength from day one. We loved talking about football and the way it should be played and he was also a bit of a Celtic fan, so I'm sure that helped to cement the friendship as well. I know he was pretty upset when I left and actually turned up at our house on the morning I was due to go to say goodbye. One of the last things I did before jetting off was to drop in at Tottenham on my way to the airport to see a few people, because things seemed to happen very quickly once Tampa had decided they wanted to sign me. Then it was off to start a new life in a new country. Of course I was a bit nervous about it all, it was a big decision for me, Myra and our kids, but it was also tremendously exciting.

The North American Soccer League was buzzing at that time. The clubs were attracting big crowds for their matches, and some of the most well known players in the game had decided to sign up with teams, either on loan deals or on a permanent basis. A few years earlier the League pulled off a coup by persuading the great Pele to play in the States and although it apparently cost millions of dollars to get him there, the move proved to be worthwhile, because he gave the whole operation the credibility it needed, and also caused the sort of excitement the game thrived on. Other top names followed, including people like George Best. By the time I arrived there was an established fan base in Tampa, and the Rowdies number one player and personality was Rodney Marsh.

I flew into Miami and then across to Tampa where I was met and put in a luxurious hotel, called The Bay Harbor. It all seemed very impressive to me. America was an exciting place and at that time, there were a lot fewer British people crossing the Atlantic. It was all very different and so was the set-up at

GORY TALES

Tampa, because I was suddenly part of a multi-national team. I'd played alongside Ossie and Ricky at Spurs, but foreign players were still a rarity in the English game. In America the opposite was the case, because they had very little home-grown talent back then, and most of the NASL players were imports. The good thing is that football and footballers are pretty much the same the world over and one of the main ingredients of any dressing room is the humour and banter that goes on. Lots of it can be childish and a bit stupid, but I always think it's good if you can have a laugh and a joke when you're at work, and it can often help to settle you into a new club. It didn't take long for the humour to start flowing when I turned up for my first day's training at the University of South Florida campus, a great facility that had everything you needed. I wasn't sure what it was going to be like in Tampa, all I'd been told was that the weather would be hot and I soon realised that was an understatement. It was boiling, but I've never minded the sun and I was delighted at the thought of training under clear blue skies. I put a short sleeved shirt on with cut-off jeans and some sandals. It was all the ammunition Rodney needed.

"Look at this," he shouted as I was introduced to my new team mates. "It's Spartacus!"

He reckoned my cut-offs and sandals made me look like someone from ancient Rome. I've actually heard him say that I had sandals that laced up to my knees, but that's typical of Rodney – he liked to exaggerate everything! I was later given the nickname of "Galloping Gorman" when I ran onto the pitch with the team. All the lads had different fun nicknames that the fans would use. But Spartacus or "Sparky" was the name that a lot of the lads used for me after Rodney's comment. It was soon clear that he was number one at the club and a lot of the younger boys were a bit in awe of him. In the time he'd been with the Rowdies his skill and ability had made him the top attraction. He was certainly a star in Tampa and I came to appreciate his talent during the time I played with him.

I couldn't help but be impressed with the set-up the club had, and with the way they looked after their players, although the luxury life at the Bay Harbor soon gave way to me having to share an apartment with two guys from what was then Yugoslavia. Zeljko Bilecki was a midfielder, and Peter Baralic a goalkeeper. They were both good lads, but hardly spoke any English at the time. Nevertheless we muddled through and it wasn't long before all three of us were straight into the season.

Gordon Jago was a good coach who had adapted to life in the States really well. He was naturally good with the media and realised that because soccer wasn't one of the main sports in the USA, we needed to be able to sell them the "product" if it was going to succeed.

Myra and I had decided not to try and sell our house in England, but instead rent it out, leaving me to start looking for a place in Tampa so that she and the children could make the move as well. We ended up in an apartment complex where lots of the other players lived. It was a nice place with a swimming pool and outdoor facilities, and I thought it would be a good start for us after the move, because there were other people with young families just like us. Poor Myra didn't really have too much of a choice because I went ahead and got us the apartment, but she was fine about what I'd done when I showed her around and we quickly made friends with our neighbours, most of whom seemed to be playing for the Rowdies. The lifestyle was different, but it didn't take too long to get used to coming home from training and going for a dip in the pool, or sitting out at night and at weekends having barbecues. There was a real range of nationalities at the club and I really enjoyed mixing with lads from different backgrounds and cultures. We had South Americans, Eastern Europeans, South Africans and Brits in the squad, including an Englishman, Barry Kitchener, who became a good friend during that first season. He was a big defender who was a legend at Millwall and a fearsome sight on the pitch, but one of the most laid-back guys I have ever met off of it. Barry came over on loan that summer and stayed in the same apartment complex.

Although it was nice living in the apartment both Myra and I felt it would be better in the long-term to look for a house, especially when we saw what we could buy out there. It was a different world. Newly built houses were so cheap, and the pound was strong at the time. We went and saw several plots of land and were absolutely delighted with what we were able to afford. A big house with a swimming pool would have been out of the question back in England, but it was a very different proposition in Florida, and we were excited at the prospect as we started to live our own little American dream.

My first home game was against the New York Cosmos, who were probably the most famous name in the NASL, and had also attracted some of the best players. I found myself lining up against the great Franz Beckenbauer and played really well, which certainly helped to settle me and allowed the fans, or "Fannies" as they were called, to see just what I could do. We also had cheerleaders who were called the "Wowdies" and they would form a path each side of the tunnel to welcome us onto the pitch. Unlike in England where the teams used to just run out onto the pitch, in the States each player would run onto the field separately with your name being announced to the crowd in much the same way as they do in American Football. There was music played at different times during the game when the action got exciting and also if a goal was scored. We also had our own Rowdie song which included the club's slogan, "Soccer is a kick in the grass!" It was all good fun and it wasn't just confined to the match itself. There would be entertainment before the games and quite often after the match was over, the crowd would stay in the stadium and the club would lay on a free concert.

The supporters were also encouraged to meet and mix with the players. There would be PA announcements about where the after-game party was going to be, which meant that a local restaurant would host a party where there would be food and drink, with the fans and players having a great time together. It helped to create a tremendous atmosphere in the City and the Rowdies became a big part of the scene, with all our matches being shown on local television.

I soon had to get used the "road trips" as well. In England an away trip was sometimes done in a day, or at most as an overnight stay. My first away trip with the Rowdies lasted 11 days. Myra actually went back to see relatives in Scotland because I was going to be away for so long and she would have been on her own. We went off and played about three games up and down the West Coast covering hundreds of miles in the process. The thinking was that it would be stupid to fly backwards and forwards, so the games were often bunched allowing you to play several teams along the West or East Coasts. America is such a vast country that even our closest matches, in places like Fort Lauderdale which was on the other side of Florida, would involve a plane journey.

The other thing I got used to was seeing a lot of familiar faces from England, especially in the summer months, with first the apartment and then our newly-built home acting as an open house for a string of visitors. We had no problem with it at all and loved seeing friends and family. Myra was the one who did all the work really, cooking meals and generally looking after any guests we had. Our families came out from Scotland and had a wonderful time including my granny, who as I've mentioned, flew for the first time when she was 92. Everyone who came out wanted the do the usual tourist things, which included visits to Disney World and places like Busch Gardens, which was a theme park in Tampa. We used to get free tickets for Busch Gardens and my dad particularly liked the place because we also got free beer. I have to admit that I went to Disney so many times I actually got sick of it, and would leave Myra and the kids to go with anyone who was over from England.

That first season in the NASL and the whole American experience that went with it was tremendous. I enjoyed my football and loved the fact that I was playing regularly once again. It also proved what I had known all along, there was nothing wrong with my knee and I had made a full recovery. I know a lot of people said that the American scene was nothing like playing in the First Division, but it was still a good standard of football, and as well as playing games, we had to train hard in boiling hot temperatures. There was no way you could have played games and not been fit.

The highlight of the season was getting to the Soccer Bowl and playing in front of 70,000 people at the Giants' Stadium in New York. It was a real shame that we lost, getting beat 2-1 by Vancouver Whitecaps, with former Ipswich striker Trevor Whymark scoring both their goals, while I got booked after a clash with Alan Ball who was also on their team. The trouble was Bally lashed out because he mistook me for our Dutch midfielder Jan Van der Veen. When he saw it was me he apologised.

"Thanks a lot Bally," I told him. "I thought you could have seen I'm better looking than Jan!"

Before leaving for the Soccer Bowl I'd had my first experience of getting a hurricane warning. They have so many of them in Florida that a lot of the people don't really think too much about it, but as we watched the weather forecasts on the television it soon became clear that they thought the Tampa area was going to be hit. As if that wasn't bad enough, we'd just moved into the house we'd had built and had to board the place up. I flew off to New York not knowing whether our lovely new home would still be there when I got back. As things turned out the hurricane didn't cause the damage they thought it would, but the thing seemed determined to get me one way or another, because when we got to our hotel in New York the heavens opened with a storm caused by the aftermath of the hurricane as it hit shore in the south of the States and moved up the Eastern Seaboard. Happily it never stopped the match from going ahead and it was a great occasion. I still look back on the Giants Stadium with fondness, because it was always a great atmosphere there and although I might have been disappointed with the result of the Soccer Bowl, I had happier memories of beating a very strong Cosmos side and getting an extra $1,000 for our efforts, thanks to the generosity of a local Tampa businessman who gave the money to Gordon as a bonus for us.

Despite the defeat against Vancouver I felt my first season had gone well and so did other people associated with the NASL, because I was selected as part of the All-Star second team, picked from all the players in the league.

The Vancouver match also marked the end of the road for Rodney Marsh. He retired as a player after the Bowl game and apart from the result, the match ended in disappointment for him when he was substituted with 10 minutes to go of the game. It was a sad end, but a week later there was a testimonial match for him in Tampa and 20,000 fans gave him a tremendous send-off. I liked Rodney but he was a very strong minded character with some people afraid to answer him back or disagree with his point of view although

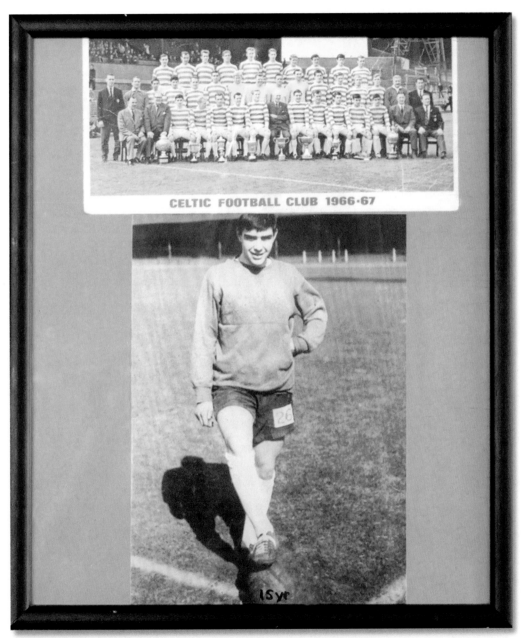

A Celtic squad picture taken at the start of the 1966-67 season, the year the club won the European Cup. That's me on the far right in the front row, and below I'm standing in front of the famous 'Jungle' terrace at Celtic Park.

Young and in love. Myra and I at a party during my Celtic days.

I had some great times at Carlisle, but we weren't exactly blessed when it came to training gear, just take a look at Stan Ternent's feet, he's the one in the striped shirt on the left, I'm wearing the number ten top.

Our wedding day. A family shot with my dad, mum and brother on the left, and Myra's parents, her two sisters and brother on the right.

A new arrival. The proud parents with baby Amanda at our house in Carlisle.

Amanda taking care of her kid brother, Nick.

Playing days with Carlisle.

My great pal Les O'Neill and I get a hug from manager Alan Ashman following promotion with Carlisle.

Happy days with Myra.

Looking forward to a new season with Spurs.

Cartoonist at work. This is me with some of the cartoons I did for the Tottenham programme while I was out of the team because of my knee injury. The drawing at the front of the picture is a self-portrait, complete with a bolt sticking out of my knee!

A visit from Myra and the kids after my knee operation which kept me out of the Tottenham side for so long.

New season, new hairstyle.
Photo call day at Spurs in 1978

A ride in a horse-drawn buggy for Myra and the kids in New Orleans during our time in the States.

Lining up in a Rowdies wall, with Wes McLeod, left, and Jan Van der Veen, right. Rodney Marsh is shouting instructions on the end.

Rowdies 1980

January

July

August

TAMPA BAY
ROWDIES

I continued my artwork while I was in America, including this 1980 calendar. The picture at the top shows me marking Johan Cruyff, while below I'm scratching my head as Keith Peacock takes a training session.

Whilst at Swindon on our way to Wembley. Celebrating our semi-final play-off win against Tranmere with Nicky Hammond and kit man Eddie Buckley, right.

We've done it! A hug for Paul Bodin after Swindon's play-off final win at Wembley.

One of my first signings as Swindon manager, Jan Åge Fjørtoft.

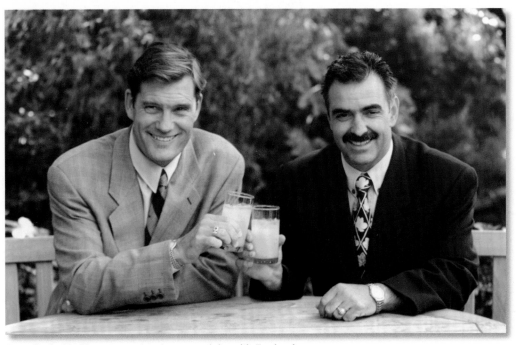

Re-united with Glenn as we toast our new jobs with England.

Training with Paul Ince, left and Ian Wright.

Final whistle in Rome. We've completed our Italian job. Next stop France.

My drawing of past England captains. Kevin Keegan, Alan Shearer, Bobby Moore, Bryan Robson, Billy Wright and Tony Adams.

'ENGLAND CAPTAINS'

Illustration by John Gorman • England Coach

Consoling Michael Owen.

With George Burley while at Ipswich.

With Glenn at Southampton.

Robbie Keane scores for Spurs.

Things not going so well, while at Spurs.

Amanda's wedding day. From the left, Nick, Myra, Rick, Amanda and Granddad holding little Aaron.

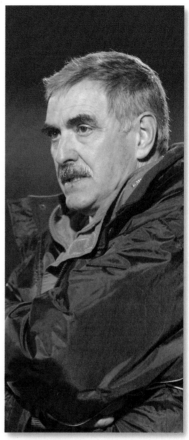

Down to business at Wycombe.

All smiles at our Wycombe Press Conference, announcing our roles as manager and assistant manager with Tony Adams.

At home with Myra and Raasey.

Holding little Aaron before Wycombe's first home game after Myra's death.

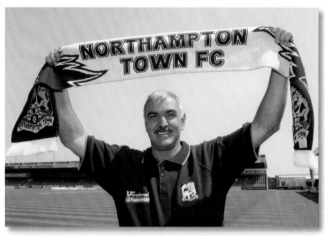

My one and only game in charge of Gillingham saw us get a vital win.

A fresh start with Northampton.

Myra managed to live long enough to see Josie. This picture was taken while she was in hospital surrounded by, from the left, Amanda, Jay, me, and Nick. With Rick and Aaron at the front of the shot.

I was smiling before the game but not after it, as Southampton were on the wrong end of a cup upset at Bristol Rovers.

there were some, like "Iron" Mike Connell, who certainly stood up to him. I think he realised pretty early on after I arrived that I wasn't going to let him get away with anything, but he did stagger me one day when I hit a ball up to him and he just refused to go for it.

"Why didn't you run for the ball?" I asked him after the match.

"It was a bad ball Sparky," he said in a matter-of-fact way. "If you want to play a ball to me make sure it comes to my feet."

I was amazed at the time, but pretty soon realised he was right. As far as Rodney was concerned if the ball was a few feet to his right or left, it was a bad ball so I quickly began to try and make sure I was more accurate with my passes and it made me a better player in many ways. Rodney was never short of a word or two, especially when it came to criticising or telling other people what they should be doing. I remember after one game we were all sitting down looking at a tape of the match to see what had gone wrong and he began shouting from the back of the room.

"Look at him," he said pointing a finger at the screen. "Why has he left his man? He should be tracking back."

"Rodney," I said. "That's you!"

To be fair to him, he took it well and had a laugh at himself. Rodney was also very good with the younger players and would always have time for them, talking about the game and sometimes showing them little things which he thought would be of help, he had quite an influence on players like Wes McLeod and Perry Van der Beck. He was an extremely skilful player and a real character who the Tampa fans loved. Rodney was larger than life and an entertainer, just like another Englishman who played for the Rowdies in 1981. His name was Frank Worthington and we became great friends during his time in Florida.

John Gorman

On the face of it we were an unlikely couple. Frank was a striker who was a real extrovert and showman on the pitch, with a love of all things Elvis Presley off of it. We were very different personalities but we just got on so well together. He came over on loan and as well as playing football, was clearly intent on having a good time off the pitch too. We ended up being room mates on the road trips and he loved to go shopping when we went to various cities. I remember one day in Chicago he managed to find a white pair of crocodile shoes and shelled out $400 for them, which was a fortune. He became a frequent visitor at our house and part of his pre-match routine for home games was to pop in to our place for some stew and dumplings that Myra would cook for him!

Frank could do things on the pitch that other players would only dream of. If you saw him in training you'd never believe he could be as good as he was, because he was never able to do the stretches we were asked to do, but if a ball came flying at him six feet in the air during a match he would somehow stick out a leg and control it. We had a lot of laughs during his time with Tampa, but there was one occasion when I thought I'd blown our friendship.

We were due to play Fort Lauderdale on a Sunday evening and had to train on the Saturday morning in preparation for the match. Frank turned up and I could smell the alcohol on his breath, he'd obviously been out the night before and then just turned up for training. I told him that he might only be on loan and treating the whole thing like a holiday, but players like me were earning our living in the States and we were professional footballers. He muttered something and then swore at me. It was the first cross words we'd had, but I thought it was probably me and him finished. That afternoon I was at home with Myra and she suddenly noticed Frank getting out of his car and walking towards the house. When I opened the door he was standing there looking a bit sheepish.

"I was out of order this morning," he said and then handed me a beautiful leather wallet he'd gone out and bought as a present to say sorry.

Other people wouldn't have owned up to being in the wrong and certainly wouldn't have been thoughtful enough to go out and buy a gift. It said a lot about his character and showed what a lovely guy he was. He played 26 games for the Rowdies and finished top scorer with 11 goals.

It was amazing how quickly we all seemed to settle in to our new life in America. Obviously the fact that I was enjoying my football helped, but it was more than that. It had a lot to do with the fact that our whole quality of life improved. We found a good school for Amanda and a good nursery for Nick, they both made friends, and so did we, including a couple, Richard and Mary Holland, who lived near us.

Richard would often be away working and I thought nothing more of it, assuming he did some sort of job that involved travel. I subsequently found out that he was with the FBI and often had to go undercover. He was involved in some pretty heavy stuff during the time we lived in Tampa, and it was certainly a very different line of work from the sort of thing I was doing. I'd go off to training in the morning and he'd go off to a drugs-bust. Paul and Joyce Posoli were another couple who were very kind to us and became great friends, while Eddie Austin who worked for the Rowdies marketing department, and Marsha his girlfriend who later became his wife, made us feel at home and were always great company.

As well as playing the regular outdoor season the Rowdies like a lot of other NASL teams, also competed in an indoor competition during the winter months. While we played in Tampa Stadium for the outdoor games, often getting crowds of 40,000, we had to go across to St Petersburg for our indoor matches which were played at the Bayfront Center Arena and had a capacity of just over 5,000.

The indoor game was fast and furious, with six players from each side on the field at any one time, but it could be a real killer. Most of the time you had a partner and the idea was that you went out and played at full pelt for three minutes, before being swapped for your partner who would come on without there really being a break in proceedings. The action was non-stop with lots of goals and I loved it. They managed to whip up a great atmosphere in the different arenas we played in and often for home games we'd make our entrance in spectacular fashion. We came on once riding in tanks, and on another occasion we were sitting on top of elephants, although I think they dropped the idea of doing it again when the club got the bill for cleaning up after them.

In my first season of playing indoor soccer, which ran through from the end of 1979 to the beginning of 1980, the Rowdies became champions. So all in all it was a great first year for me, I'd reached the Soccer Bowl, been part of a Championship winning indoor team and was named in the All-Star second team selections.

Another Englishman arrived at the club just as we were about to embark on our indoor season in 1979. Keith Peacock who had a long and distinguished playing career with Charlton, joined the Rowdies as Gordon's assistant and became a big influence on the team. Keith was a good coach and got on well with the players, he was able to cut across any language barriers and worked hard with the team, making sure training was always interesting and enjoyable. I got on well with him from the very first day he arrived and because there was very little between us in terms of our age, I think we probably had a lot of common ground. Keith, his wife Lesley together with their children Lauren and Gavin soon settled into life in Tampa and the family became friends of ours. Gavin later went on to have a tremendous career as a professional footballer back in England, with Newcastle, Chelsea and QPR among others and is now a football pundit for the BBC, but when he first moved to Florida he looked the epitome of the all-American kid. The good thing was that he was still able to play soccer and did well for a team called 'The Black Watch.' He was only about 11-years-old at the time but was a fine little footballer.

Although I loved playing I had always had an interest in coaching, going right back to the days when I was a teenager at Celtic. Back then I'd coached a kid's team and Myra used to come along to our midweek sessions to help out. The idea of one day becoming a coach was always in the back of my head and while I was at Tampa I would often go and help out after the main training sessions had finished.

I used to like working one-on-one with some of the younger players, helping them to improve their game. One day Keith was watching me and came over to say that he liked what he'd seen me doing.

"One day I'll have you working with me John," he said. At the time I just smiled and thought no more of it, but the thought obviously stuck in his head and it was Keith, a few years later, who gave me my first break in coaching.

That first season was probably the most successful the club had during my time with them. I had four very good years with the Rowdies and managed to maintain a level of consistency that proved beyond doubt there had been no lasting problem with my knee. In 1981 I was named in the All-Stars first team but a year later, with the NASL not quite the force it had been when I first arrived and with changes at the club, including a new American coach

John Gorman

called Al Miller, it was time for me to move on and concentrate on the indoor game which was attracting a lot of interest. I had my last season with the Rowdies in 1982, the NASL wanted to make sure that more Americans and fewer foreigners were playing for the teams. I was 33-years-old and knew that my time in the outdoor game was coming to an end.

I'd had a great time with the Rowdies and was lucky enough to be playing when the interest and the crowds were still there. I could also appreciate the way that they marketed the game and how they tried to sell it to the American public. It wasn't an easy thing to do because American football, baseball, basketball and ice hockey are established sports out there. Soccer still hasn't managed to make the same impact in the States as it has in the rest of the world, but even when I was out there it was clear that it was becoming really popular with kids of both sexes. Since then there have been some very good American players who have come through and played at the top in our own Premier League as well as in Europe while women's soccer has been tremendously successful. However the fact remains that the game still seems to lag behind the other four major sports that I have mentioned.

In the 1970's it was Pele and his involvement in the NASL that really brought the league to life, and encouraged other big names to follow him. I suppose that the MLS must now be hoping David Beckham has a similar effect, and if some established international players begin playing in the USA, I'm sure there is the potential for it to grow. Certainly at grass roots level there is no problem at all, and if the college kids come through and have a strong league to play in the game might begin to flourish.

Back in 1982 the big thing in US soccer was the Major Indoor Soccer League, because it was so fast paced and guaranteed to be high scoring I think a lot of Americans enjoyed it more than the outdoor 11-a-side game. I certainly liked playing it even if the matches were very physically demanding. Tony Simoes was the new manager of Phoenix Inferno and he had seen me play the indoor game during my time with Tampa. He obviously thought I could do a job for him because he made a bid for me and pretty soon I was off across America with Myra and the kids having to suffer all the disruption to their lives that went with a move from Florida to Arizona.

It looked as though there was a good set-up at the club and I also discovered there was a bit of a Scottish connection. The general manager was a guy called Norman Sutherland, who was from Edinburgh, while fellow Scots Willie Watson, Peter Miller and Lawrence Tierney were playing for them and before I went there my old Celtic team mate Vic Davidson had been part of the team, as well as Peter Marinello, the former Scotland and Arsenal winger. There was another familiar face in the Phoenix ranks, because my old Tampa buddy, Jan Van der Veen, was there too.

So after four years in Tampa we rented out our house, loaded up our car and headed west. We even took our cat with us on a trip that lasted four and a half days. At one point somewhere in Texas the cat got out and wandered into a field as we stopped to have a break at the roadside. I had to climb over fences and walk across fields to retrieve the family pet, but did the return journey a bit faster when I got chased by a bull. The cat also managed to have a pee over Myra, while Nick was sick over my shoulder as I was driving down the freeway. We eventually got to our hotel in Phoenix and met Willie the next day. He showed us around and took us to see a complex which ended up being the place where we initially rented an apartment before buying a house later during my time with the club.

We quickly felt comfortable in Phoenix and made friends. The children settled in well and Myra was very happy with the house we bought and even

John Gorman

started playing indoor women's soccer. The only slight problem came with my wages which could sometimes be late and the players got word that there might be some financial trouble at the club. At one point we were told that instead of going to the Inferno's offices to collect our money we all needed to troop down to the airport to meet a guy who would pay us. Sure enough, when we got there a guy met us with a briefcase and then proceeded to pay us our money. I think we all thought it was a bit strange, but the main thing was that we were getting paid and it was in cash. This whole thing went on for a while, but then we were told that new owners were coming in with a lot of money to spend and they had some new ideas for the club. So the regular trips to the airport stopped and we waited to see who was going to take over. To our surprise it turned out to be the Mormans, and although they were happy with the Phoenix part of our name, they insisted that we change the 'Inferno' to 'Pride.' We had been used to running out onto the indoor pitch through an archway of flames, but once the Mormans took over it was a giant lion that greeted us. They did a good job in upgrading everything at the club and we had great offices and a new indoor training complex. As I have said, the trips to the airport also stopped and we found out that there had been some kind of mafia connection involved previously, which was why our money was paid in cash, and the reason for us having to go to the airport was because the guy had just flown in from another part of the States and it was probably mob money!

The MISL season was in the winter months and to supplement my income during the summer I began running soccer camps with Willie Watson. It was something I had started during my time with the Rowdies after they had stopped playing indoor games, and I thoroughly enjoyed it. We also found time to take a break and go back to Tampa, unfortunately we were stopped in El Paso on the way back as part of a routine border check looking for illegal immigrants. Although we were coming from the east, the town straddles Texas, Arizona and Mexico.

When I could see we were going to be stopped I told Myra not to panic, because although we had nothing to hide and had applied for our Green Card, which was a document allowing you to stay and work permanently in the States, it hadn't yet been granted and I'd heard from some of the other lads that border checks could sometimes be awkward if you got the wrong guy.

"Let me do the talking," I said. "If he asks you anything just say 'Yup' or 'nope' then we can't go wrong."

It was soon a case of famous last words, because as soon as the border guard started firing questions at us about our nationality, Myra blurted out that she was Scottish. It's all very well being proud of where you come from but there's a time and place! In fact, I think she was just too honest for her own good, but I'm afraid honesty did not prove to be the best policy, because we were hauled out of the car and placed in a hot and sweaty holding room while we were given the third degree. They were pretty nasty and even made threats about taking the kids away. It was obvious they thought we were illegal immigrants, and the whole business only stopped when Myra managed to find a receipt in her bag detailing the fact that we were applying for a Green Card.

On the playing front things were good, and I loved the indoor game, especially when I played as a goalkeeper with licence to attack. It was a ploy used by sides when they needed goals and I scored a few during my time with the team, but like any football club you never know what is around the corner, and one day we were all summoned to a meeting called by the guy who was, in effect, the chief executive. He told us that Tony was no longer going to be our manager.

"I want Willie Watson and John Gorman to be player-assistants, and do you know who's going to be the new manager?" he asked. "Me!"

I don't think any of us could believe it, but worse was to follow. The next day we were out on the training pitch and he turned up to take the session dressed in a suit. It was as if he was off to work in a bank, not coach a bunch of footballers. He did have some background in sport, but unfortunately it was all in basketball and his tactics for a match reflected that. The trouble was that in one of his early games we were losing 4-0 and eventually pulled it round to win 5-4, mainly because of the players and not his management, but he was hailed as a hero.

If his appointment as manager came as a bit of a shock to us all worse was to follow in the summer of 1984 when I got a phone call telling me to come down to the club offices and collect my last pay cheque. The club had folded. It was a real blow, not just because I wanted to play football, but also financially. We'd bought a house in Phoenix, a house in Tampa and still had one in England. There were mortgages to be paid and I suddenly had no money coming in.

We had to try and sort things out quickly and sure enough that's just what we did. We managed to sell the house in England in a day, while it only took two weeks before we had a buyer for our place in Phoenix. It meant that we had to rent somewhere and move all of our stuff out of the house, or more precisely, Myra and the children did, because I left them for a month while I had one last chance at trying to sort out a new club for myself

In the end I was given the chance of a trial with Tacoma, another indoor team, near Seattle in Washington State. I went there with one of my Phoenix team mates, Argentinean Ruben Astigarraga, who had been promised a contract. The team had former Birmingham manager, Freddie Goodwin, in charge with ex-Arsenal full-back, Bob McNab as coach. I saw it as another opportunity to play football and so I was prepared to give it everything I had. I did the full pre-season with them, including a 10 mile run in the hills which had poor Ruben claiming the English were crazy because of the way they trained. I also played matches for them as part of their build-up to the new season, but after a game in Las Vegas I was pulled aside and told they weren't going to offer me a contract. It was all done in a very nice way, but I realised that was it, my playing career was over and I'd better start getting used to it.

CHAPTER 7

ATLANTIC CROSSING

I suppose it was quite sad when the day actually arrived and I knew that was me finished as a player, certainly as far as America was concerned, I didn't really have time to sit and dwell on it.

I knew I had to return to Phoenix and help organise our move back to Tampa. There was really no where else we could go. We'd settled in well during our time in Arizona and it was particularly hard for the kids because they had made some very good friends, but I had to start earning money away from the game and decided I would do that in Tampa. We headed back east with Myra driving one car full of some of our possessions, while I drove another car with a trailer attached carrying more gear. She had one of the children with her and I had the other one. It was another four and a half day trek, during which time we broke down in Texas and I almost fell asleep at the wheel, using the old matchstick trick to try and keep my eyes from closing.

When we did get back to Tampa we had to rent a home because our own house was still being rented out. I started a business with another guy doing painting and decorating, before branching out on my own. I had little cards printed to advertise what I did, because as well as painting houses I also did some artwork and ran a soccer camp. The cartoon I drew for my business card showed me with a paint roller in one hand, an artist's brush in the other, while at the same time juggling a football. Talk about jack of all trades! But I did get work with most of my money coming from painting houses, and Myra got a job doing secretarial work. I'd earned good money in the States but we certainly weren't in the sort of bracket where I could afford to sit back and live off my investments. I needed to work and that's what I did.

While we'd been in Phoenix I'd received a call from my brother Joseph telling me that my granny was pretty poorly, and the general opinion was that she might not pull through. Everyone in my family knew how close I'd always been to my gran and so I flew back with Myra and the children expecting the worse, but when I went to see her she seemed to perk up and soon after began to feel better. I was delighted that she'd managed to pull through and flew back to the States marvelling at what a tough and determined lady she was. Nevertheless, I was realistic enough to know that she couldn't go on for ever. So when I got a call from my mum sobbing down the phone one day after we'd returned to Tampa, I immediately thought granny had finally passed away, but the news was in fact far more shocking. It wasn't my grandmother who had died, it was my brother Joseph.

His death was a complete shock to everyone, because there had been no hint of it happening. It was a real tragedy for his wife Sheila and four children,

John Gorman

Stephen, Desmond, Keiron and Louisa. I found it difficult to come to terms with, particularly as he was just 38-years-old at the time. We all flew back for the funeral and within a matter of months, were making a similar trip once more, when my granny finally passed away. I'm sure the shock of Joseph's death contributed to her health taking a turn for the worse, and suddenly the idea of staying in America seemed less appealing to me. The deaths of Joseph and my grandmother had made both Myra and I feel that we wanted to be closer to home and the relatives and friends who were there, but I also knew that if I was going to go back I needed a job. After finishing playing I realised that although I could earn a living from painting houses and running soccer camps, my real ambition was to make it as a coach.

I began to contact friends in the game back home and let them know that I would be interested in returning to coach in Britain. Lots of people said they'd love to have me working with them if something came up, but I knew it wouldn't be easy for me and realised I had to be prepared to be patient.

Meanwhile, in 1986 at the age of 36 I got the chance to play for the Rowdies again, when an anniversary game was organised between players from the club's glory years and the US national team in Tampa Stadium. Rodney Marsh had come back to the club as manager in 1984 and although the NASL was a thing of the past, the club operated as an independent team for two years before joining the American Indoor Soccer Association for one season, and later carried on in various guises before folding in 1993. The anniversary game was really enjoyable and both Glenn and Ossie came over and played as guests for the Rowdies in front of 25,000 fans. It was a great way for me to end my time in American soccer and in the summer of that year, an old friend proved to be as good as his word when he gave me the chance of a job back in England.

GORY TALES

I mentioned earlier that Keith Peacock had told me when he was coaching Tampa that he liked the way I worked with some of the younger boys after training and that one day he'd have me working with him. Keith had been one of the first people I had contacted when I made the decision to return home. He was manager of Gillingham at the time and had done a really good job with the club. He promised to keep me in mind and also said that if he heard of any other jobs that he thought I would be suitable for, he would put my name in the frame. Apparently Frank Clark, the Orient manager, was looking for a youth team coach and Keith recommended me. Frank was all set to give me a chance with him when Keith found he suddenly had a vacancy of his own. Ted Buxton who was scouting for Keith at Gillingham, got the opportunity to go to Tottenham as their chief scout. Instead of going for a straight replacement Keith decided he would beef up his coaching staff and offered me a job looking after the youth and reserve teams. He told me the money wasn't too good, but it was the chance for me to take my first step on the coaching ladder and I happily accepted.

If it had all been about money I would never have said yes, because I knew I would be returning to England earning the same as I did when I was at Carlisle 10 years earlier, but I was just happy to be given the chance and it's something I have always been grateful to Keith for. He was a smashing bloke to work for and I got involved in everything pretty much from day one, including coaching the youth team, driving their mini-bus and playing for and coaching the reserves. At the ripe old age of 37 I even turned out for the first team, coming on as a substitute in a 6-0 Littlewoods Cup defeat at Oxford, and then starting in the line-up for the return leg which we drew 1-1.

It was pretty hectic right from the start but I loved it. Once again I had done my usual trick of leaving Myra and the children while I took off for my new job. She and the kids ended up getting back into our own house in Tampa, but when the time came for them to follow me to England and our new life in Kent, the children got really upset. Not surprisingly they had made a lot of friends in the States but there I was dragging them back to England. I think it was a particular wrench for Amanda, who was just entering her teens. Both her and Nick were very young when they went out there and a lot of their formative years had been spent there. They'd been in America for more than seven years. Both of them were used to the American way of life, and it was certainly going to be very different in England. They'd obviously visited Britain during the time we were living in Tampa and Phoenix, but actually moving back was a tremendous upheaval for them. I don't think it did them any harm in the long-term, but at the same time I now appreciate how difficult it must have been for them to re-adjust and make a whole new set of friends.

There was a real difference in my own lifestyle as well, because when I first arrived at the club I stayed with Keith and his family, but then ended up living in digs not far from the club ground. I was so busy with my new job that it really didn't matter too much because I was hardly there. The trouble was that even when Myra and the children arrived from the States we had to rent something before finally buying a house in Lower Halstow.

Gillingham might not have been a big club but it was a great little set-up with some good players like striker Tony Cascarino, who went on to play for Chelsea, Celtic and the Republic of Ireland, at the club. Keith had done a very professional job in improving everything from the youth team to the first 11. He also had an excellent assistant manager in Paul Taylor and a guy called Bill 'Buster' Collins whose official title at that time was 'trainer.' Buster was one of those football people who had been around a long time at the same club and had done a variety of jobs. He was sort of 'Mr Gillingham.' I got on well with him and found him a great help.

That first season saw Gillingham finish fifth in the old Third Division, which meant they went into the play-offs, but the system wasn't the same as it is now and Gillingham then had to face Sunderland the team which had finished third from bottom of the Second Division on a home and away basis. We did brilliantly in the first leg winning 3-2 and then after a real battle at their place the match ended 4-3 to Sunderland, sending Gillingham through on the away goals rule. The final was against Swindon and it was also over two legs. The first finished in a 1-0 home win for Gillingham, while the return saw Swindon edge a 2-1 victory, forcing a third game between the sides which was played at Selhurst Park. It was a really tense affair and Swindon came out on top with a 2-0 win, sending them up into the Second Division.

The result was a real disappointment for the club and it would have been fitting had Keith managed to take the club up, because he'd worked really hard during the time he'd been in charge since coming back from Tampa. From my own point of view things had gone pretty well for me in my first season. I loved working with the kids and the reserve team. I was learning all the time which was perfect for me and the reason I'd come back in the first place.

There seemed a lot to look forward to in the next season despite the disappointment of the play-offs, and when the first team recorded two incredible early victories lots of people began to think the club were in for another promotion challenging season. Towards the end of August 1987 Gillingham had beaten Southend 8-1 at home and then a week later managed to top that with a 10-0 home victory over Chesterfield.

They were amazing results, but the team hit a bit of a sticky patch and slipped away from the main promotion contenders. By the time Christmas came around they were mid-table and Keith had asked me to do some scouting for him and take a look at Southend, who were going to be the opposition for a match at their place on New Year's Day.

Southend were playing at home against Bristol Rovers and that same morning Tottenham had a home game against West Ham. Nick was a real Spurs fanatic and I arranged for us to watch the game, and then I planned on going to Southend for their match with Rovers. When it was half-time at White Hart Lane I suddenly heard someone talking about the other morning kick-offs.

"Southend are winning 2-1," said a guy sitting behind us.

I was suddenly in a real panic. I'd assumed Southend were playing in the afternoon. I was supposed to compile a report for Keith and I hadn't even managed to get to the match! I decided to drive to Aldershot where the first team were playing and make my apologies to him personally. This time the game was in the afternoon but Nick and I still didn't manage to get there until the break, by which time things were not looking good. Gillingham were losing 5-0, not the best time to let Keith in on my little cock-up with the Southend fixture. Things improved in the second half, but the first team still ended up losing the match 6-0. That night Keith phoned me up but it wasn't to pick my brains about Southend, instead he told me that he thought he was going to get the sack. I was amazed because although the team hadn't been doing too well and were on the wrong end of that 6-0 result, I still felt Keith had done a tremendous job and would have got the team up there challenging again given time. He told me to be at the ground the following morning and sure enough Keith was right, but there was a bit of a twist in it all for me. The club wanted Paul to take over as manager and me to become his assistant. Keith insisted that we should go ahead and take the opportunity, but in my own mind I felt as though I wasn't really ready for the job because I had only been coaching for 18 months, but in football you often have to grab chances when they come along and I couldn't really turn it down.

Both Paul and I were thrown in at the deep end and we managed to get the team up the league to ninth place before falling away towards the end of the season finishing 13th in the table. That summer both Paul and I did our full FA coaching badges and George Burley was on the same course. He'd had a bad knee injury while playing for Sunderland, but looked terrific whenever he was taking part in some of the sessions, and was certainly fit enough for regular first team football, as he proved after signing for us and being an ever-present in the league for the Gills the following season.

Paul and I were really looking forward to putting our stamp on the team in what was going to be our first full campaign in charge, but all the optimism and plans were brought to an abrupt halt in late October, when Paul was given the bullet and I went along with him. The team hadn't been doing well, and after a decent start we began to lose games. After eight consecutive league defeats the directors had decided they'd had enough and it was time for a change. It was a shame for Paul because he was desperate to do well in the job, but as often happens in football, he wasn't given time to try and turn things around.

He was very unhappy about having to go, and I remember how he drove his car up on the pavement outside the ground, scattering the waiting reporters who were trying to grab a word after he'd got the bad news. On that very same evening I got a phone call from Keith Burkinshaw, who wanted to pick my brains about the Gillingham players and the set-up at the club. It was pretty obvious to me that he was going to become their next manager.

"What are you doing tomorrow?" he asked me.

John Gorman

"Keith, I've just got the sack so I'm not doing anything," I told him.

He asked me to meet him at the club the next day to have a chat, which is exactly what I did. I thought he wanted more information and I was happy to pass on my opinions and anything else he might need. The official announcement hadn't been made but as soon as I saw him I realised he was going to be the new man in charge. After we got over all the pleasantries Keith came straight to the point. He said he was going to be the new Gillingham manager, but then completely surprised me with what he said next.

"I want you to come back to the club," he said.

I was absolutely amazed. One minute I was being sacked by Gillingham and the next I was being asked by the new manager if I wanted to come back. I know football can sometimes be crazy and that you should always expect the unexpected, but there was no way I could ever have been prepared for a turnaround like that. The first thing I did was contact Paul to tell him what had happened. He told me to go ahead and take the job, saying that I was settled and had kids at school in the area, and also pointing out that just because they had sacked him it didn't mean I should say no to a good opportunity.

Although Keith had been the person who had effectively ended my playing career at Spurs, I certainly didn't hold any grudges, and when I'd been back from the States during the American close-season, he had let me train with Tottenham and virtually admitted he'd made a mistake about my injury. We got on fine and I had a lot of respect for him as a coach and a manager, so I said yes and found myself back at Priestfield Stadium once again.

Not too long after Keith had taken over I was in his office one day putting away lots of my scouting reports when the telephone rang and Burky asked me to get it. Keith Blunt, who had been involved with the youth team at Tottenham was on the other end of the line and wanted to speak to Burky. The conversation was short and sweet and after it ended I asked Keith what Blunt had wanted.

"He wanted to talk about the assistant manager's job," Keith said in a very matter-of-fact way.

"What assistant manager's job?" I asked him.

"The job here," said Keith.

I couldn't believe my ears and let Burky know exactly what I thought of the idea and of him. He told me he wanted me to stay on as chief scout, but I was 39-years-old and wanted to learn more about coaching. Being a chief scout was no good to me at that stage in my career and so I was off once more. It had been short and not too sweet second time around.

I found out years later from Keith that the reason he'd wanted to bring in Blunt was because he'd been told by old Buster that although I was a good coach I was a bit too soft with the players. Burky felt he needed someone who was going to be tougher on the training pitch, but things didn't work out too well for Gillingham that season because they ended up getting relegated to the Fourth Division, and Damien Richardson took over as manager from Keith Burkinshaw at the end of the campaign.

I was out of work with no money coming in and no real prospect of a job on the horizon, but although I was getting near to my 40th birthday, I was still fit and still loved kicking a ball around just as much as I did when I was a kid back in Scotland, so I decided to dust off the old boots and began playing non-league football for Sheppey. I think I got about £50 a game, but I loved every minute of it and played with a great bunch of lads. It was a decent standard and very enjoyable, but I knew my future was in coaching and I had to try and get back into it as soon as I could.

I managed to do just that very quickly thanks to Bernie Dixon and Frank Clark at Leyton Orient. I had got to know Bernie because he was the club's Youth Development officer and obviously I'd come close to joining Orient after leaving America. I was invited down for an interview and Frank offered me a job looking after the youth and reserve teams. Once again it involved a bit of everything, and once again I enjoyed it tremendously. The only thing that was a bit of a problem was the travelling. On a good day I could leave my house in Kent and be at the training ground in just over an hour, on a bad day it could take four times as long. I often used to stay overnight, not in a hotel but in the boardroom.

If the youth or reserve team had been playing an evening game and we got back to the club's Brisbane Road ground late, I would sleep on a couch in the boardroom rather than trek all the way home and have to be up early for training the next day. I also used to drive the mini-bus and do a bit of scouting. On a Saturday I'd watch the youth team, wherever they were playing, and then be off scouting. Once again it was a great learning experience and I had some very good young lads playing for me in the youth team, players like Chris Bart-Williams and Adrian Whitbread. I was also left alone to get on with things, which was nice for me and good of Frank who was always very encouraging, although there was one occasion when I thought I'd over-stepped the mark.

I was in charge of the reserve team and we had a young goalkeeper with us on trial. Before the match I'd told the keeper to make sure he tried to throw the ball to his full-backs whenever he could, so that we could build play from the back and keep passing the ball. At half-time during the game Frank and his assistant, Brian Eastick, came in and took over. Frank absolutely slaughtered the poor keeper, telling him he should be kicking the ball out and not throwing it. After the team had gone back out for the second half I pulled Frank aside and told him that I didn't want my team playing that way, I also said that if he wanted them to knock the ball long then maybe he should take the team instead of me.

"You better come and see me in the morning John," he said.

I thought he was going to give me a real telling off for what I'd said, but when I turned up the next day to see him Frank said he'd given the whole thing a lot of thought and told me to carry on playing the way I wanted to.

"It's your team and you're in charge," he insisted. "Keep playing the way you want to play."

I thought it was a great way for him to handle the situation because he would have been quite within his rights to have told me I was out of order and I should do what he said, but Frank was a good man manager as well, and he liked to give people the chance to get on and do their jobs. I just can't stay quiet when it comes to something I feel strongly about, and I spoke up again one Christmas when hampers were being given out by the club. I asked why the youth players didn't get anything because they were probably the ones who needed it most. The chairman, Mr Wood, obviously agreed with me because he later came back with a pile of cash, giving me £50 for each player. He was a really lovely chairman and helped create a good atmosphere at the club. In my first season with Orient Frank guided the first team to promotion to the Third Division via the play-offs, and the chairman made sure we were all given a bonus.

I enjoyed being involved in lots of different things, just as I had at Gillingham and once more my overall coaching experience was getting better, but it wasn't great for my family life because I was away such a lot. Myra never

John Gorman

complained and I think she could see just how much I enjoyed the job. I was dealing with youngsters from the age of about 11, right through to established professional players. Although my main responsibility was for the youth team and reserves, I would also take a look at some of the evening training sessions for kids, making a note of those I thought had the potential to go on and be signed at youth level. One little kid who I remember being very good for his age was the son of a guy called Steve Shorey, who used to scout for Orient, his son was called Nicky who went on to make a name for himself with Reading in the Premier League and also play for England. He was an obvious talent then and it's been nice to see him do so well.

Although I'd had my 40th birthday I still played in the reserves sometimes as well as being in charge of them. The team would often be a mixture of youngsters coming through, and more established players who had perhaps been dropped from the first team. While I was working at Orient Glenn was over in France playing for Monaco, having left Tottenham in the summer of 1987, but there was still a strong Hoddle connection for me, because his younger brother Carl was at Brisbane Road and often played in the reserve team. Glenn even came over to watch him play once and I was in the same side. In the summer of 1990 the World Cup took place in Italy with Scotland due to play one of their group matches against Brazil in Turin. Glenn had suggested that me, Myra and the children visit him in Monaco, and then drive across the border and up to Turin for the game. So we loaded up our car and set off for the South of France, stopping on the way before reaching Monaco and being met by Glenn. He hadn't been playing for Monaco because he was waiting to go into hospital in an effort to sort out a knee injury, but he knew I'd want to see the training and arranged for Nick and I to sit in on an afternoon session being held by the Monaco manager, Arsene Wenger. It was the first time I had ever met him and I immediately liked the man. He was charming and Glenn had told me just what a good coach he was. My opinion of him has never changed, and his achievements at Arsenal are phenomenal. I love the way he wants his teams to play football, always ready to pass and move the ball around. He will never compromise his beliefs and Arsenal have been transformed under him, playing some beautiful stuff in recent years. Not an easy thing to admit for a Spurs man like me!

When Arsene found out that I wanted to see the Scotland game he immediately said he would arrange for some tickets for Glenn, Nick and me, so on the day of the game the three of us together with Myra and Amanda trundled off in my car into Italy and onto Turin. The weather was absolutely awful and it was pouring with rain for the whole journey. When we got to the stadium the car park was in a real state and was awash with water. There were trams and coaches arriving with Scottish fans and we actually helped one fan who was in a wheelchair. As we lowered his chair to the ground he looked over his shoulder and recognised Glenn.

"F*****g Glenn Hoddle," he said looking a bit surprised and bemused. He didn't bother saying thanks, and you could tell he wasn't about to ask for an autograph either!

Brazil won the game with the only goal of the match nine minutes from time, and we found out later that Myra and Amanda had abandoned their plans for a shopping trip because of the rain and instead watched the whole of the game on a giant screen outside the stadium, but despite the terrible weather it was a great experience to be at a World Cup Finals, even as a spectator. Of course, I could never have known at the time that I would get another chance to go to a World Cup tournament eight years later, and in very different circumstances.

John Gorman

Glenn's wife, Anne, together with their daughters, Zoe and Zara, had gone back to England because they knew Glenn was about to go to Germany for the operation on his knee. They had a beautiful apartment which overlooked the sea, and he suggested that we stay on while he was away and use it as a holiday base, which was perfect for us and we had a great time out there. One night before Glenn left for Germany he and I sat up into the small hours just talking about football. It was one of those things that might sound boring to a lot of people, but we loved every minute of it and it was soon clear we both had very set ideas on the way we liked teams to play. I was telling him all about my experiences with Gillingham and Orient. I said it had been a great learning curve for me and opened my eyes to the way things happened on the coaching and managerial side of the game. He had obviously picked up a lot from Arsene and loved the way he allowed his side to play and express themselves, but within a disciplined format which allowed the team's good football to have an effect. It was a lovely chat and I think in many ways it laid the ground for what was to happen with both of us during the years that followed. One other thing Glenn did that night was ask me a question.

"John," he said looking a bit awkward. "Are you all right?"

I knew immediately what he meant. He realised I wasn't exactly earning bundles of money and that things had been a bit tight since coming back to England. It was his way of asking whether I wanted any help with my finances, and it was typical of him. There was no way I was going to take any money from him, but it was a terrific gesture and the sort of thing that only real friends would ask.

After my little summer jaunt to France and Italy I came back to England refreshed and looking forward to the new season with Orient, little knowing it was to be my last with the club.

GORY TALES

That season there were two Hoddles to be seen at Leyton Orient. Following the operation in Germany Glenn had tried desperately to get fit enough to resume his playing career and after leaving Monaco, he would sometimes use our facilities to help him along. The club's physio, Bill Songhurst, was very good at his job and I think everyone was amazed at how hard Glenn worked when he came in to do his sessions.

I continued with my work as youth team coach and also looking after the reserves, playing whenever necessary. Towards the end of the season the reserves had a game against Arsenal which was due to be played behind closed doors at Brisbane Road, and the day before Glenn called and said he had some news and wanted to talk to me about it. He explained that he'd been offered the manager's job at Swindon and that if he took it he wanted me to go along with him as his assistant. It was obviously quite an exciting prospect, but not the sort of thing you wanted to discuss on the phone and so we arranged to meet the next day when both Carl and I would be playing for the reserves. Glenn said he'd come over and see me after the match, so I played the game and then slipped out to have a chat with him in his car.

We talked the whole thing over and I decided it would be a great chance for both of us, but I knew I had to let Frank know and wasn't sure what his reaction would be. After all, he'd given me a chance when I was out of work and had let me get on and run things the way I wanted. He'd been great to work for and I felt a bit awkward about having to tell him I wanted to go, but I had no need to worry. When I told him he couldn't have been happier for me, realising that it was a chance to improve my career. We shook hands and I left the club without any arguments or squabbles. It had been a smashing place to work, but I now had the prospect of a whole new challenge waiting for me. I was approaching my 42nd birthday and the move couldn't have

John Gorman

come at a better time. When I'd told Myra about it, she was all for it, giving me the sort of encouragement she always had, but once again I knew it was going to mean another family upheaval, with me having to live away from home initially.

Glenn and I were due to be in charge of our first Swindon game in a home match against Watford at the end of that week. Two days before, on a Thursday morning in early April, we made our way down to the club for the announcement about us taking over. On the way there we stopped for a coffee and I bought a newspaper.

"Glenn, have you seen where Swindon are in the league?" I asked.

"No," he said.

"They're seventh from bottom!" I told him.

He'd been so excited and keen to take the job that Glenn hadn't even realised we were going into a club with a relegation battle on its hands.

CHAPTER 8

PARTNERS

Swindon might have been struggling near the foot of the Second Division but we knew we'd inherited a club with some good players in it who must have been desperately disappointed not to have been playing their football in the First Division.

Less than a year before we took over Swindon had won the Second Division play-off final at Wembley with a 1-0 victory over Sunderland, but little over a week later they were relegated to the Third Division when the club admitted 36 breaches of league rules, including 35 involving illegal payments to players. The punishment was later reduced on appeal, and the club were allowed to stay in the Second Division, with Sunderland taking their place in the First Division. It must have been a terrible blow for the team and for our old mate, Ossie Ardiles, who had led them to the Wembley win in his first full season in charge. Ossie had moved on to take over as the Newcastle manager, leaving the vacancy at Swindon that Glenn filled.

Ossie had the team playing in a cavalier fashion which was great to watch and produced some fantastic football for the Swindon fans to enjoy, but after the success of that first season, there had obviously been a bit of a hangover and the side were struggling to put some decent results together. We took a training session on our first day and it went really well, but my overall impression was that maybe the players could have been a bit fitter. Our first game in charge wasn't too successful with Watford winning 2-1, leaving us in no doubt at all that we had a real challenge on our hands if we were going to avoid the drop. In fact we only managed to win two and draw one of our remaining seven league games that season, but it was enough to keep the team up, finishing 21st in the table. We knew things had to improve dramatically in the next season and both Glenn and I were confident that would happen.

We had some quality players in the squad, people like Colin Calderwood, Paul Bodin, David Kerslake, Micky Hazard, Steve White and Ross McLaren. We even had, Nesto Lorenzo, a World Cup finalist. He had been part of the Argentina team beaten 1-0 by West Germany in the 1990 final in Rome. He was a good player, but wasn't used too much by Glenn because he just seemed to like bombing forward. He was a centre-half who wanted to play like a centre-forward and consequently would leave you exposed at the back if he had his own way.

We also had another decent player available at the start of our first full season in charge – Glenn. He had managed to get himself back to match fitness and played in a sweeper role, which he took to like a duck to water. He was able to read the game and then use his ability with the ball to get things moving for us and set up attacking plays. With Glenn having to keep himself fit because he was still playing, it meant I had the opportunity to learn a lot about the management side of the game as well. I think we both enjoyed working with each other, and the chemistry seemed to be right, mainly due to the fact that we already knew each other so well. The team stayed in or around the top places, but as the season drew to a close we struggled to make a final push and missed out on a play-off place by five points, finishing eighth, but we'd added to the squad and knew there was potential there. We had also got the team playing the way we wanted and felt things could only get better the next year.

Having shuttled backwards and forwards like a yo-yo for a time from our place in Kent while I lived first in a house and then a flat, Myra had eventually moved west to join me in a house which we rented from the club, but by that time things had changed a bit on the home front. At the start of the 1991-92 season I made one of the saddest journeys of my life when I had to take Amanda to St Mary's college, Strawberry Hill. Of course I was pleased for her as she started her studies in sports science, but like any other dad, I couldn't help feeling sad about my little girl leaving home. I'm not ashamed to admit that I sat in the car crying my eyes out after I dropped her off. Like all kids she had grown up faster than I could ever have imagined, and it seemed such a short time since I used to push her pram around in Carlisle after training.

We went to Holland as part of our pre-season in the summer of 1992 and won the tournament we were competing in. There was a good feeling about the club when we kicked off for real with a 1-0 home win against Sunderland, who had only lasted one season in the top division before being relegated. Glenn scored the winner in the second half, and we started the campaign well. By mid-November we were second in the league and playing some lovely football, with Glenn hardly missing a game as he continued playing in the

John Gorman

sweeper role. We'd strengthened the side with some bargain buys, getting in people like midfielders John Moncur and Martin Ling, as well as striker Dave Mitchell. All of our exploits, both on and off the pitch were being filmed for a documentary, and they got plenty of good footage as the team played well and stayed in the hunt for promotion, but despite looking as though we might manage to go up automatically, we had to be content with the play-offs after finishing in fifth place.

Lots of people have described the play-offs as a lottery and to some extent they are, but despite failing to win any of our last four matches, we still went into them with a lot of confidence. After beating Tranmere 3-1 at home in the first leg of the semi-final that confidence seemed well founded, but the return was a very different matter and we only just managed to scrape through with the home side winning 3-2 on the night in a really dramatic game. John Moncur gave us the lead and we thought we were cruising, but then Tranmere came back and went in front before Craig Maskell equalised for us with nine minutes to go to the relief of all of us. That relief lasted exactly two minutes, because Rovers got a penalty which Kenny Irons scored from and it was a nail-biting few minutes for me on the touchline before the referee finally blew his whistle.

We'd made it through to the final and for the second time in three years the club had the chance of top flight football for the first time in its history, but the rewards this time around were much greater because the Premiership had started a year earlier and the money available for competing with the best clubs in England was staggering. Leicester were the other team to make it through to the final and they were desperate to make amends for missing out at the same stage 12 months earlier when Blackburn beat them 1-0. We took the squad away to Bournemouth for a few days as part of our preparations in the week leading up to the final, and although we weren't over confident, there was a feeling that it was going to be our year. The only real distraction came from the rumours which had started to surface regarding Glenn's future with the club, with stories in the press linking him with Chelsea. It was no surprise that the press were speculating about his future. After all, he'd done an outstanding job with a small club who had limited resources and the type of football we were playing was getting rave reviews.

We stayed at Glenn's lucky hotel, The Marriott near the M4, on the night before the final and although I suppose there must have been some nerves, everything seemed very relaxed and we were all very positive. That mood continued the next day when the team walked out at Wembley, and we couldn't have got off to a better start. Glenn had scored a great goal in our first game of the season to give us that win over Sunderland, and in what was our last match of the campaign he gave us the lead to settle the team down. We went in 1-0 ahead at half-time and when Craig Maskell and Shaun Taylor scored in the second half it looked as though we were on course for the Premiership, but things can change so quickly during the course of a football match as we were to find out to our cost.

Leicester somehow managed to score three goals in the space of 11 minutes to completely change the complexion of the game. We'd been in control of the match but all of a sudden we found ourselves on the back foot, with Leicester understandably full of confidence having managed to turn the match around. Brian Little was the Leicester manager at the time and he told me later that he couldn't believe how cool I seemed during a game which was such a see-saw affair.

With six minutes to go Steve White, who I'd sent on as substitute for Craig Maskell, was fouled by the Leicester goalkeeper, Kevin Poole, and we were awarded a penalty. If I'm honest I'd have to say that I wasn't really sure it was

John Gorman

a foul, but we got our spot kick and Paul Bodin stepped up to score what proved to be the winner. As the final minutes ticked away I turned around to see our Physio, Kevin Morris, crying his eyes out. He had been at the club for years and was Swindon through and through. The emotion was just too much for him and he couldn't believe his team were actually going to get into the Premiership, it meant so much to him. There was a real feeling of relief when the final whistle blew and then the celebrations began. It was a wonderful day for everyone connected with the club, and when you saw all the Swindon fans it made you realise how important it was for them. They could start to plan their trips to places like Manchester United, Tottenham, Arsenal and Liverpool. They were about to rub shoulders with the big boys and I don't think a lot of them could believe we'd finally done it.

The strong rumours that Glenn would be moving on continued before the final at Wembley and after we'd got promotion. By the time we had our civic reception, riding through the town on an open top bus, word had got out that he was going to be on his way to Chelsea and I think people assumed that if Glenn went, I would be off too. There was one guy who seemed to follow the bus as it crawled through the crowds and he popped up at several different points during the ride. Each time he appeared he would stick an arm out pointing at me and say the same thing each time.

"You're going nowhere, You're going nowhere!" he shouted at me.

The reality was that things all came to a head very quickly, with Chelsea coming in for Glenn and myself. I decided it was a great opportunity and agreed to go with Glenn, despite the efforts of Rikki Hunt, who was managing director of Burmah, the club's sponsors and an associate director of Swindon. He had meetings with us and tried to get us to change our minds, but we both felt the time was right to move on and eventually all that was left for us to do was pay a last visit to the club and say our goodbyes.

It was a shame because we'd both grown to really love the club and had enjoyed a lot of success there. They were good people to work for and the supporters had been fantastic. Glenn had shaken hands with everyone and wished them well. I went upstairs to collect the last of my things and we agreed to meet a bit later because we were due to go and see the Chelsea chairman Ken Bates. As I was about to leave, Ray Hardman, the Swindon chairman, asked if he could have a word.

"John, I know Glenn is going," he said. "But I want you to stay and be our new manager."

To say I was taken aback would be an understatement. It was just something I'd never contemplated, but it soon became clear that Ray and the rest of the board had given the matter a lot of thought and they wanted me to take over. He was determined to win me over and spent about half an hour trying to convince me to change my mind about going. I explained that it wasn't something I could make an instant decision about and asked him to give me some time to think it over. But on the way home as the offer started to sink in I began to feel that staying would be the right thing to do. It was a chance for me to be a manager in my own right, and the more I thought about remaining with Swindon, the more I felt comfortable with the idea. The first person I wanted to tell was Myra. When she picked the phone up I think she was expecting me to tell her everything was sorted out and I'd signed a contract with Chelsea.

"Myra, the chairman wants me to take over as manager from Glenn," I told her. "So I've decided to stay."

"Oh, no!" she replied. From her tone, I could tell she thought I must be stark raving mad.

CHAPTER 9

GOING IT ALONE

The other person I had to contact was Glenn, and I knew he wasn't going to be too pleased with me.

He'd left Swindon's ground thinking I was on my way to Chelsea with him, and as you can imagine he was stunned when I told him what had happened and that I'd decided to stay and become the new manager. It wasn't a pleasant call to have to make and Glenn obviously felt let down by me and what I'd done. I realised that I'd let my heart rule my head, because although I was going to get my first job as a manager and it was going to be in the Premiership, I also knew just how tough it was going to be. There was very little time to do anything before the new season because the summer break was so short. The club couldn't really plan for the future until they knew which league we would be playing in and with the play-off final coming at the end of May, it meant that you were trying to play catch-up on so many fronts. I also realised that despite the extra money that would be coming in because of our promotion, there was no way Swindon were awash with cash and it might be hard attracting new players to the club. I had to smile to myself as I drove home and remembered what I'd said to Glenn when we'd decided to leave and go to Chelsea.

"Glenn," I said, thinking about how difficult it would be for anyone coming in. "Whoever gets the job is going to be right in the s**t."

That person turned out to be me! It was quite clear from the way my phone call to Glenn ended that he was very upset about the whole thing, and it was probably the first time we'd ever fallen out. A lot of people seemed to think we stopped talking to each other, but that never really happened. We had been mates for a long time and he knew I'd always been my own man. I made the decision to stay and after he got over the disappointment of it we talked to each other throughout the season that followed. Neither of us was ever going to let something like my change of heart stop us from being friends. The other call I made was to Ray Hardman, telling him that I'd decided to say yes to his offer and become the club's new manager. He was delighted and invited Myra and I to have a meal with him that night, giving me the chance to talk things over with him and begin planning for the new season.

One of the first things I had to do was decide on who I wanted as my assistant, and I turned to my old friend, Davie Hay, who I knew had good experience as a manager himself having been in charge of Celtic and St Mirren as well as being an assistant manager at Motherwell and Watford. I trusted David and realised his experience could be invaluable, but I'm not sure the job really suited him in the end. He'd been used to being a manager and perhaps being an assistant wasn't quite right for him at times, but I was glad he was there and I think the board felt we would make a good management team.

Another one of my early moves came in the transfer market when Norwegian, Jan-Aage Fjortoft, joined us from Rapid Vienna for a club record fee of £500,000. It was a huge amount for a club like Swindon to pay at that time, but I knew that if we were going to compete in the Premiership we needed some proven quality players to help us. Jan was a classy striker and showed just how skilful he was from the first day he arrived. He did some great things in matches and was a smashing lad, the trouble was that he never made the kind of impact in front of goal that I had hoped for and failed to find the back of the net in a league match until January.

We began the season with a 3-1 defeat at Sheffield United and then lost at home to Oldham by a single goal before getting beaten 5-0 by Liverpool in our next match which was also at home, and 5-1 at Southampton. What a welcome to the big league.

We did manage to pick up our first point of the season following that Southampton game, when we drew 0-0 at Norwich, and it was obvious to anyone who watched us that we were a good footballing side. We played with real flair, which pleased me and was a treat to watch at times, but despite good draws with West Ham and Newcastle, by the time the end of September came around we were bottom of the table and people were already saying that we had no chance of staying up. I knew that the odds had been stacked against us from the moment we'd gained promotion at Wembley. We were a small club and just getting into the Premiership was a remarkable achievement, but the one thing I was determined for us to do was have a go at the opposition in every game. I wanted us to play football, and I wanted the players to express themselves and not be afraid.

GORY TALES

When we went to play reigning champions, Manchester United, at Old Trafford they were already at the top of the league and would go on to record back-to-back Premiership titles. I stood in our dressing room before the game and started to read out their team. It was packed full of star names like Steve Bruce, Paul Ince, Mark Hughes, Roy Keane and Eric Cantona. Suddenly I just screwed the piece of paper up and threw it on the floor, leaving my players looking bemused at what I'd just done.

"Look," I told them. "We all know they've got great players so what's the point of me reading their names out and going through the team. Let's just go out there and have a right good go at them."

I got a great response from the lads that day, but although we scored twice in the second half after trailing 2-0 at the break, we still came away having been beaten 4-2. It was no disgrace to lose to them and we had gone out and played good football, but the fact of the matter was that although we could sometimes dominate games, we were getting caught too easily and were leaking goals.

Throughout the season I recall having a lot to be proud of despite the defeats and set-backs we suffered. One great moment for me was going back to White Hart Lane with my own team and getting a 1-1 draw against a very good Tottenham side who were managed by Ossie Ardiles and loved to pour forward in great numbers and attack teams. Towards the end of November we picked up another point in a home game with Ipswich, but it was only our sixth point in 15 matches, and we still hadn't managed our first win in the league. We needed to stick three points on the board quickly and four days after that 2-2 draw with Ipswich we were due to play QPR in another home game.

On the Monday after the Ipswich match the weather turned a bit frosty and

John Gorman

I decided that I would take the boys who had played in the game on a short run in the country near our training ground. I told Davie Hay to take the rest of the first team squad and give them a good session and that I'd be back with the others later on.

We had a good run in a place called Aldbourne, which is not far from Swindon, and just as we were coming to the end we passed a pub. I honestly don't know why I did it, but I stopped outside and then told the boys that we were all going to go for a drink.

As you can imagine, it wasn't the sort of thing they'd expected two days before a home game, during a season in which we couldn't seem to buy a win, but they certainly didn't need too much persuading. So we all trooped into the pub, still sweating from the run and still in our training gear. Heaven knows what the landlord thought when he saw the Swindon first team up at the bar ordering drinks. I told them all that it was on me and then ordered some lunch as well. I also phoned Davie to tell him to bring the other lads down and we stayed in there for some time sinking quite a few beers during the course of a very long lunch. Our training session turned into a boozing session and I think a few taxis were needed to ferry people home. It was a spontaneous thing and I was convinced it would do no harm at all when it came to team morale.

I had read that about a year earlier Dave Bassett, who was the Sheffield United manager, had organised a Christmas party for his players just a few days before the season. He thought his side were a bit of a second half team, not in individual matches, but taking the season as a whole. It was as if they really only got down to business in the second half of the season, once the Christmas festivities were over. The trick seemed to work for Dave, because just a few days after his party, his side beat Manchester United 2-1 at home in their opening game of the season. Just as we were leaving the pub that day I called the landlord over and asked if he could lay on a Christmas lunch for all of us the next day, which is exactly what he did. I told our directors what I was planning and they backed me by saying they would pay for the lunch. So 24 hours later we were all back in the pub, but this time there was no alcohol consumed because the QPR game was coming up the next day. We had the whole works. There was turkey, Christmas pudding and the pub was decorated for us as well. Everyone had a great time and I kept my fingers crossed that our 'early Christmas' would produce the same effect it had for Dave and his team, but within 10 minutes of the start against QPR my heart sank. Luc Nijholt came sliding in for a tackle and was immediately shown a red card by the referee. We were down to 10 men and I thought my master plan had been thrown well and truly out of the window. Later in the first half we got a corner and Keith Scott, who I'd bought from Wycombe to try and get us a few goals, popped up at a corner and scored. The place went wild and somehow we managed to hold on to that lead for the rest of the game. It was like the Alamo at times, but we did it and as a result got our first ever Premiership win. The fans celebrated as if we'd won the league and there was a real sense of relief all round, but once the euphoria had died down I knew the real trick would be building on the result.

In our next five games we played some good football and got a couple of draws one of them was a 2-2 result against Liverpool at Anfield and we were actually clapped off the pitch because of the way we'd played. We followed that with another win, when we beat Southampton 2-1 at home. Games and results like that breed confidence and despite the fact that we were due to face the mighty Arsenal in our next match a day after Boxing Day, there was a real feeling that maybe we could do something against them.

John Gorman

One of the players I'd brought in was Terry Fenwick, he was an experienced defender with a bit of steel about him and had played at the highest level, including being capped by England. Terry did well for me early on and was a strong personality in the dressing room. I had no problem with that, in fact I signed other more experienced players during that season, such as Brian Kilcline.

But the trouble with experienced players is that you also get opinions. They are more inclined to feel able to question what you're doing as a manager and sometimes their influence with younger players can have a real effect. For the Arsenal game I decided that I wanted to play with three at the back. I felt the Gunners just had too much pace for us with the likes of Ian Wright and Kevin Campbell. When I told the lads what I was planning they didn't like it. We'd played with a flat back four in other games and for the only time in my career I let myself be influenced by them and relented. We'd play with a four, but at the same time we would play our football from the back and be aware of the threat they posed because of their pace.

The game turned out to be a disaster for us with Campbell scoring a hat-trick and Wrighty getting another goal when he hit a looping ball over Fraser Digby in our goal. Final score, 4-0 to them and I was not a happy bunny. Not because of the result, which was bad enough, but because the players had completely disregarded what I'd said about the way I wanted them to defend.

"Your off-side plan didn't really work John, did it?" One press guy asked me after the match.

"It wasn't my off-side plan," I said bluntly.

The players had gone out and done their own thing, taking it upon themselves to try and play with an off-side trap that had proved to be a disaster. I was annoyed with them and let the players know how I felt, but at the same time you can't afford things like that to fester at a club. The thing to do is move on and make sure it doesn't happen again, and the good thing was that 48 hours later we were in action again, when we travelled to play Sheffield Wednesday. Once again I was furious when the final whistle blew, but this time it had nothing to do with my players. They had performed really well and earned a 3-3 draw, it was the referee who upset me. Wednesday had scored a goal while our keeper, Fraser Digby, lay injured on the floor after being clattered. In the end, after twice leading the game through Andy Mutch and Craig Maskell, we had to be grateful for a 90th minute equaliser from Maskell to earn us the draw in a game we should have won.

The old saying that when you're down the bottom, nothing seems to go your way certainly seemed to be the case for us, but there's nothing you can do about it except keep believing in yourselves and in what you're trying to do. I knew that whatever happened I wasn't going to compromise on the way I wanted the team to play football, and despite being at the bottom of the table there were successes.

At the end of January and beginning of February we had back-to-back victories when we played Tottenham off the park at our place and won 2-1, before following that up with another home win, beating Coventry 3-1. But then we lost 5-0 at Aston Villa and drew at home with Norwich. Our next game was away to Manchester City and the trip produced drama both on and off the pitch, neither of which was particularly pleasant for us.

On the night before the game we stayed at Mottram Hall, which is a lovely hotel with beautiful grounds and a golf course, the ideal place to prepare for an important game, and the City match certainly came into that category. We might have been at the bottom looking up at all the other clubs, but City manager Brian Horton and his players were under pressure too because they were only a couple of places above us. The pressure was on for both sides and a lot was made of it in the press, claiming it was a must-win game.

After checking in to the hotel we had our evening meal and then all went to bed to get a good night's sleep before the big game. At about 4am in the morning I was woken up by someone banging on my door, and when I opened it I saw the hotel manager standing there with a guy who turned out to be a senior Manchester police officer. It was pretty clear from their expressions that they'd come to see me about something serious. I was still sleepy after being disturbed but then the police chief gave me some news which had me awake in no time. He told me they were investigating claims of a possible rape. Apparently a girl had been found wandering in the grounds of the hotel and I think she had been pretty drunk. She and her friend had been with a group of lads and made some claims about what had gone on. Her friend hadn't come back, and the police were looking for her.

David Hay and I had to go with the manager and the policeman as we knocked on all of the player's doors to see if any of them had a girl in their room. They were all fast asleep and didn't know what was going on when we woke them up. Some of them said the next day that they thought they'd been dreaming. Once they'd checked the player's rooms, they let us all go back to bed while they continued to look for the missing girl. At about 6.30am I got another knock and opened the door to find the policeman there again. They'd managed to locate the girl and found out from her that the group of men her friend had told them about were actually at a party in a house near the hotel. Whatever had gone on happened there and didn't involve any of my players, but because the first girl had been found in the hotel grounds they assumed it had happened on the premises. She'd told them about a group of young lads and because there was a football team staying at the hotel, the players became possible suspects.

The game itself probably summed up what had been happening to us throughout the season. After finding it hard to score in the first half of the season, Jan Fjortoft began to hit the back of the net with the sort of regularity I'd always hoped for. He got his first league goal in the win over Tottenham and then followed it up by scoring all three goals against Coventry together with two more in the 3-3 draw with Norwich. He opened the score for us at City and then hit what we all thought was our second. So did the City keeper because he booted the ball up field in disgust, but the linesman had flagged and the 'goal' was disallowed. It was a bitter blow especially as they went on to equalise when Kevin Horlock put through his own goal later in the first half, before David Rocastle scored their winner. The next day Dave Bassett rang me up.

"I'm sorry John," he told me. "You're going down. I was at the game and any team as unlucky as you were has got no chance!"

I knew exactly what he meant but there was no way I or any of my players were going to throw in the towel. If I'm honest, I knew we were going down but we certainly weren't going to do it without a fight, and we were going to continue to play our football. We did it in the game at Newcastle and looked really good, but once we conceded a goal the floodgates opened and we were beaten 7-1. After the game I was asked by a reporter if I was going to quit.

"Are you going to quit?" I asked him. Of course the answer was no, and I was just making the point that despite a bad result and a tough season there was no way I was going to walk away from the job, even if that job was a really tough one at times, and as if to prove that point our next match was a home game with Manchester United.

Before meeting us they were due to play a mid-week game at Old Trafford

John Gorman

against Sheffield Wednesday and I decided to go and watch them, taking Nick with me. They put on a great performance and won 5-0 with Eric Cantona scoring two of their goals. So we'd just conceded seven goals, and they'd just scored five by the time we met at Swindon's County Ground. Perfect.

I knew lots of people thought we were on a hiding to nothing, but I wanted us to really take the game to them, just as we had at their place. Cantona was an obvious threat, a great player who could unlock any defence in the world if he was in the mood. I managed to bring in another experienced player, Lawrie Sanchez, from Wimbledon, and gave him the job of looking after Cantona. Lawrie did really well and clearly managed to frustrate the Frenchman, who got himself sent off after stamping on John Moncur. I usually say "hard luck" or something consoling when an opposition player gets sent off, but as Eric marched towards the touchline his eyes were full of anger, and I decided it might not be a great idea to say anything to him. We got a 2-2 draw with them and after the game Moncur went and asked Cantona for his shirt. He gave it to him as well – even signed it for him!

Our last away game of the season brought our first away win and it came at QPR, the same team who'd provided us with that famous first Premiership victory. I was pleased for our fans who had travelled to the match because they had something to celebrate, even though we knew we were going down. We'd had terrible problems all season with injuries to our goalkeepers and it continued to the very last game which was at home against Leeds. I'd got Paul Heald in on loan from Leyton Orient, but he'd broken his wrist and had to play the match with strapping. We lost the game 5-0 which meant we had conceded 100 goals during our season in the top division. It's not the sort of record you want to be remembered for, but anyone who saw us in the Premiership will know we played attractive football and tried to provide entertainment, which is something I will always be proud of. The players gave me all they had and I couldn't have asked for more.

As soon as the season was over I went off on a golfing trip with my old mate Les O'Neill, who had joined Swindon as chief scout when Glenn and I took over. We travelled to France from Plymouth for an organised golf event, which I thought would be a good way for me to unwind following all that had happened during the season, but it rained for the whole time we were there and I arrived back in Plymouth without ever hitting a golf ball. The Swindon directors had asked to see me at a hotel in Bournemouth and as I drove along the coast for the meeting I became increasingly uneasy about what was likely to happen. After all, we'd just been relegated and I thought that would probably be it for me because of the way football works, but I was wrong. The chairman said they'd liked the type of football I had tried to play but at the same time made the point that we had to learn from the mistakes as well. The outcome of the meeting was that they wanted me to carry on as Swindon manager and I was delighted to do just that, but I also knew the expectation levels of everyone connected with the club had risen. Promotion a year before had been a fantastic thing and a season in the Premiership had whetted everyone's appetite for more.

We had a good pre-season which included playing a tournament in Cyprus. I worked the players hard during the trip and wanted to make sure we approached it in a professional way. The players were allowed to have a few beers after the games, but then it was back to the hotel and we always trained the next day. After one of the games one of the lads asked if some of the senior players could go out for a few drinks and I said no. I later found out that despite what I'd said some of them had gone out after all. When we got back to England the directors wanted to see me because word had got back

John Gorman

to them that the players had been out on the town during the trip. It was a silly incident and the sort of thing that happens at football clubs all the time, but I felt I was under pressure right from the start of the season.

When we did kick-off the new campaign we really hit the ground running, and by the end of September we were third in the league. We had also managed to see off Charlton in the Coca-Cola Cup, after two great games which saw us lose the first leg at home 3-1 before winning 4-1 at their place in extra-time. It was a big contrast to the previous season and naturally everyone at Swindon was delighted.

At the beginning of October we played Wolves at home in a league game. They were top of the table at the time but we pulled off a terrific 3-2 win. It seemed as though everything was beginning to go right after all the disappointment of relegation. I played golf with the club's vice chairman, Mike Spearman, on the Monday after the match, before leaving to watch our reserves play that evening. When I got back to my house Kevin Morris's daughter was waiting for me. She said her dad hadn't been seen since Sunday and they were all a bit concerned. I didn't know where Kevin was but told her not to worry and that I was sure he was alright.

The next morning when I arrived at our training ground the place was swarming with cars and the press were out in force. I soon found out why. Kevin was dead. He had committed suicide and been found in his car somewhere in the countryside. Like everyone else I was stunned and couldn't quite believe what I was being told. Kevin had been at Swindon forever and was part of the fabric of the place. I remembered how he'd cried on the bench at Wembley as we gained promotion and I knew that the club and his job meant so much to him. There were no real signs that he was upset or depressed enough to take his own life. He did always worry about losing his job as physio, and had mentioned it not only to me but to Glenn, Ossie and even Lou Macari when he was manager of Swindon. I'd told Kevin that whatever happened I would always find him something at the club and he was a lovely man who everybody liked.

The news was shocking and affected the whole club. We were due to play Portsmouth four days later and I told everyone to go home and we would meet up again on the Friday. There was no point in training because nobody would have been able to concentrate. We played Portsmouth and it was a cracking game but we lost it 4-3 and I could tell a lot of the lads didn't really have their minds on the game. We were in fifth place after the match, but then went on a terrible run, losing five of our next six games including a 3-2 defeat at Bristol City. After the game I went to see my old friend Joe Jordan who was in charge of his first game since taking over City. Joe asked me how I managed to get Swindon playing the way we did. Our football had been great once again, but we'd ended up getting beat.

"Thanks very much for the compliment Joe," I said. "But I think I'll be out of a job tomorrow."

He thought I was being stupid but I knew that the recent run we'd had was the sort of thing that can get a manager the sack. I had a funny feeling about it because usually win, lose or draw a few of the Swindon directors would pop their heads around the dressing room door, but against Bristol City they had been conspicuous by their absence. Sure enough I later got a call asking me to go into the club the next day and I was told the board thought it was best that I leave. The club acted properly when it came to sorting out my contract I had with them and there was no animosity.

As the saying goes, "the only thing certain in football management is the sack," and when it happens you just have to dust yourself off and get on with it.

CHAPTER 10

ENGLAND'S SCOTSMAN

One of the other things that I've heard said so often in football is that, "you never know what's around the corner." That was certainly true in my case as I contemplated life without a job.

The first thing I did after leaving Swindon was take Myra away for a short break in Tenerife. After all that had gone on I thought it would do us both good to have a change of scenery and have time to think about what we wanted to try and do. We could have only been on holiday for a day or two when I got a phone call from Joe Jordan who had tracked us down and wanted to have a word with me. I explained that we were having a short break and he asked if we could talk properly once I got back to England, which was exactly what happened. When I had my meeting with Joe he asked me if I fancied joining him at Bristol City as his assistant.

I liked the idea of working with him and Bristol wasn't a million miles away from Swindon. By this time we'd sold our house in Kent and were renting a property in Swindon, Nick was in college and it meant we didn't have to uproot ourselves, which was good for the family. It also meant that I would quickly be back in the game, working with someone I knew as a friend and who was also a very good coach. Joe allowed me to get involved in most things that went on, including the coaching and I also took the reserves and did a lot of scouting.

It was a good club and I quickly struck up a rapport with the fans. Joe was a smashing boss to work for and liked to do things in a very precise way. He was very hard working and expected the people around him to be the same, which was no problem at all for me. I quickly got into the job and would quite often go out in the city for a meal with Myra after matches or even stay overnight in a hotel. But although I liked Bristol neither of us ever really thought about moving there, and we didn't feel that Swindon would be the right place for us to make our next house purchase either. We would often go for a meal in the Bracknell and Ascot area with our friends, Dave Deller, and his wife Mal and Glenn and his wife Anne, who also lived nearby. For some reason we just fell in love with the area and both Myra and I decided that if we got the chance we would try to buy something there. Until that time came I was quite happy to stay in Swindon and commute to Bristol.

When Joe joined City they were struggling near the bottom of Division One and we were never able to get them away from the relegation zone. In the end the club dropped into Division Two and ironically they were joined by Swindon. They had been 16th in the table when I left them but eventually

John Gorman

finished two places above City in 21st place. Nobody likes to get relegated and that was certainly true for City and although we didn't start the new campaign in Division Two very well, things began to improve in the second half of the season and the team started to move away from the danger zone. By the time April came around there was no real danger of dropping into Division Three, but at the same time a late promotion challenge was unrealistic as well and it seemed as though the last two months of the season would wind-down without any real excitement for me. I was happy and enjoyed the job I was doing, even though it often involved a lot of travelling because of the scouting Joe asked me to do.

One evening I was due to watch a game at Brighton and decided to give Glenn a ring to ask if I could stay with him after the match because I wanted to break my journey back to Swindon and take a look at houses in the Bracknell and Ascot area. When he answered the phone Glenn seemed a bit distant and distracted, but said it would be fine to stay. The next day he introduced me to a guy who knew all about property in the area. I looked at some in Ascot but decided they were out of our price range, and then he told me about an old farmhouse in a place called Binfield which he'd heard about. I went to see it and immediately fell in love with the place and its location. The house needed work done on it, but it was perfect and I phoned Myra to tell her I'd found our dream home. When she saw it Myra felt exactly the same way I did, after all the years of travelling because of the various moves I'd made I think we both felt that we finally wanted to put down some roots in a place we truly felt would be our home. Berkshire to Bristol isn't exactly an easy commute, but I still felt it was worth it, and we put a deposit down on the house that very afternoon.

Not very long after all this happening I was due to watch a double-header for Joe. An afternoon game involving Reading reserves and an evening game between Oxford and Chelsea reserves. On my way from Bristol to Reading I stopped at my house in Swindon and for some reason Glenn chose to call me on my home phone.

"John, I need to have a word with you," he said. I told him that I was on my way to Reading and then I was going to watch his reserves against Oxford that night.

"Forget tonight's game," he insisted. "Come over to my house because I need to see you."

I agreed to cancel my trip to Oxford and said I'd be over after the Reading match finished. On my way to the game I phoned Myra and told her that I thought Glenn was going to offer me a job, which was strange because I knew Graham Rix and Peter Shreeves were already doing a good job there. She told me not to be silly and said that although we'd remained friends, he was unlikely to give me a job after what had happened at Swindon. I could see her point but at the same time I knew Glenn and I was convinced he had something for me at Chelsea.

When I got to his house Glenn opened the door and there was a bit of small talk before he sat me down, offered me a cup of tea and then hit me with the news he had been so eager for me to hear.

"John I've got something to put to you and it'll be a bit of a surprise," he said.

"Go on then, tell me," I replied wondering exactly what he was leading up to.

"I've been offered the England job and I want you to be my assistant."

"Are you sure?" I asked. "I'm Scottish for a start and I've never been an international player."

"Don't worry about all of that," he insisted. "I want you as my assistant and I know we'll do well together. We're right for it."

John Gorman

I'd gone to Glenn's house thinking he might want to give me a job coaching Chelsea's reserves or youth players and suddenly I was being offered the chance to help coach the best players in England. It didn't take me too long to make a decision.

"All right," I told him. "No problem!"

Glenn then told me why he'd appeared a bit distracted on the phone when I'd called to ask to come over and stay following the game I'd watched at Brighton. Apparently just before I rang he'd been contacted by Jimmy Armfield to sound him out about the possibility of becoming England manager. It was an amazing coincidence.

Once Glenn had told me and made it clear that he thought I was the right man for the job it was one of the easiest decisions of my life, but I knew I still had to break the news to Joe and the Bristol City board. He had thrown me a lifeline when I was out of work after being sacked by Swindon and I was very grateful for that, but when I did tell him he was fine about the whole thing, except that as a proud Scotsman he probably wondered what the hell I was doing! The Bristol board were brilliant about it as well. In fact they were proud that their assistant manager was going off to work with England, and they made the whole thing very easy to handle.

My last game with City was an away trip to Carlisle in the final game of the season, there had already been speculation in the press about Glenn taking the England job and two days before we played Carlisle he officially accepted the post, with people speculating on who he might take with him as part of his backroom staff. Not too many people thought I was in the frame, some believed we had never really patched things up after Swindon, which of course was nonsense, but perhaps the main reason nobody thought I was a likely candidate was because I was Scottish. Anyone who knows me will tell you

GORY TALES

that I am as proud to be a Scot as anyone north of the border, but as far as I was concerned this was all about football. It was a chance for me to work with and coach some great players and to be involved at international level. I saw it as a marvellous opportunity and a wonderful job, both of which proved to be the case.

When it was finally announced that I would be Glenn's assistant I think a lot of people were surprised, but both Glenn and I were comfortable with the situation and so were the FA, who were going to be employing me to help look after their national team. Before I was officially appointed Myra and I went to Tenerife for a short holiday, and it was while we were out there that a story broke at home saying I would be teaming up with Glenn. A day after the report we bumped into Nicky Summerbee, who had played for me at Swindon before going to Manchester City. He told me that some West Ham players, including two more former Swindon lads, John Moncur and Adrian Whitbread, were having a drink in a nearby bar and suggested Myra and I should go and say hello, which was what we did. We had a couple of drinks with them all and they'd obviously heard about me getting the job with England. Julian Dicks was one of the West Ham lads who was there and he had a pretty severe short hair cut. At some stage Myra jokingly ruffled what hair he had on his head and made some funny comment about it. We were all having a laugh and the drinks were flowing so we left them to it and went back to our apartment before returning to England a few days later.

Soon after we got back I went to Liverpool to watch one of the Euro '96 games because the finals of the Championship were being staged in England. It was a great chance for Glenn and I to look at not only all the England games, but also matches involving other sides we knew we would soon be meeting in qualifying games for the World Cup in France two years later. We

John Gorman

were going to be thrown in at the deep end come September when we started with a qualifier against Moldova who along with Poland, Georgia and Italy were in our group.

It was Italy who I had gone to see at Anfield because they had two matches there in the space of three days against Russia and then the Czech Republic. The day after watching Italy play I bought some newspapers and couldn't believe my eyes. There was a story with Dicks basically saying that I'd told him he'd never play for England because of his hair cut! It was totally ridiculous and I'd said nothing of the sort. The only Gorman he'd really talked to that day in Tenerife had been Myra and she certainly hadn't said he wouldn't be playing for England, but there it was in black and white. It was a stupid thing, but at the same time it made me realise just how big and high profile the job of working with England was going to be.

Although Glenn and I had been officially confirmed as the new England management team, we weren't going to be taking over until after Euro '96, and Terry Venables was still in charge for the tournament. As I've mentioned, we were able to watch all the England games, but were pretty much kept at arms length by Terry. We never really got involved with the players in any way as England played their matches, one of which was against Scotland at Wembley. As you might imagine I came under the spotlight a bit for that game because of my background. Who was I going to be supporting? That was the question being asked. The fact was that I could watch the game as a fan, because I wasn't actually involved with the England team at the time. If I'm honest, I also have to say I was delighted we never played Scotland during the years which followed when I was part of the England set-up.

England beat Scotland 2-0 that day and when Paul Gascoigne added to Alan Shearer's opening goal, I know there were quite a few photographers trying to get my reaction to what had happened. It was also a game which saw England's challenge for the Championship really take off. After that win they put on a tremendous performance to defeat Holland 4-1 and move into the quarter-finals where they needed penalties to beat Spain. Their Championships came to an end in the semi-final when they missed out against Germany in a penalty shoot-out. It was a sad end to the tournament, but at the same time England's performances had lifted the country and with it the expectation level for what the team could do going into the World Cup qualifiers.

I loved seeing all the games during the tournament, including the final which saw Germany beat the Czech Republic 2-1, a game I was lucky enough to watch from the Royal Box with my family, although I'm not sure Rick would have been too happy with the huge smile Czech goalscorer, Patrik Berger, gave Amanda as he climbed the stairs to the box after the match!

Once the tournament was finished it was time for us to really get stuck into the task of planning England's future. Glenn and I had already talked a lot about the way we would go about the job, and part of that meant finding out as much as we could about the opposition. Our first qualifying game was going to be away against Moldova in September, followed five weeks later by a home fixture against Poland. We obviously wanted to have a look at the opposition first hand and managed to take in a double-header, watching Russia against Poland, before flying on to Bucharest for a game between Romania and Moldova. We flew in a small plane from Moscow to Bucharest and were met on the tarmac by some characters who looked liked they'd stepped out of a Mafia movie. In fact, they were just government officials and we were whisked straight through customs and were looked after really well for the entire time we were in the country.

John Gorman

We watched the game sitting next to the former tennis star Illie Nastase, who immediately recognised Glenn and started talking football to the two of us. It was all a long way from what I'd been used to, and I couldn't help smiling to myself when I realised that only a few months earlier I'd been compiling scouting reports on sides in Division Two. It was a different world and I loved every minute of it.

I also thoroughly enjoyed taking my first training session. It was great to be working with the cream of English football. People like Alan Shearer, Ian Wright, Tony Adams, Paul Gascoigne, Paul Ince, David Seaman and Teddy Sheringham, all big names in the game but some of the nicest guys you could wish to meet and it was a pleasure to coach them. Once again I think there were those who wondered how they would respond to me, but I can honestly say that from the very first day I took training, until the last time I was in charge of an England session, there was never a problem. They were all totally professional and at the top of their game, they understood the need for good training and I don't think the fact that I was Scottish ever came into it. In fact, many of the players were used to hearing a Scottish voice on the training pitch, because they were at clubs with coaches or managers who came from north of the border.

Moldova was a real eye opener for all of us. We were there to win a football match in the first of the qualifiers, but I think the first thing which really struck us all was the degree of poverty we saw when we arrived. The lads actually dipped into their own pockets for a collection to help a local children's home, and I think we all found the whole experience a bit of a culture shock. The game was played in Chisinau and we were treated really well while we were there, but one of the biggest problems during any trip abroad for a football team can be boredom. Players like to have things to do after they train and on the night before the game we thought it would be a good idea to take the squad to watch our under-21 side in action against their Moldovan counterparts. The England team won 2-0 and the match managed to make headlines in the national papers back home, not for football reasons but for something which happened off the pitch.

We had all been watching the game when it suddenly started to rain. The only real shelter available was a small area that was being used by the press and it had a tiny roof on it. As soon as the rain began we all made a dash for it, but you had to climb some steps to get into the sheltered area. Just as Paul Ince started to make his way up, Paul Gascoigne grabbed at his tracksuit bottoms and pulled them down. The trouble was it wasn't just the tracksuit which ended up around his ankles, because his underpants came down with them. A photographer managed to snap the moment and the picture duly appeared in the newspapers the next day, with a shot of me laughing my head off in the background. Some of the papers were saying that I was supposed to be in charge and yet look how England's finest were behaving, with me looking as though I was part of the whole thing as well. As far as I was concerned the incident had been funny, it was another 'Gazza moment' and the lads were all laughing at it as well.

Incey proved to be a great asset during my time with England. He was magnificent in so many of our games and the sort of player you always want in your team. I got on well with him and had a lovely meal with him and his wife Claire once when I went over to Italy to check on his fitness and form during his time with Inter Milan. I also got to see the Milan players training under Roy Hodgson, who was the manager at the time and he really looked after me well.

Ince, along with a young David Beckham making his full international debut, were part of the team which took to the field to play Moldova the night after the under-21 game, and helped us record a vital first win in our group, with a 3-0 victory. A few weeks later at Wembley we managed to sneak a 2-1 win against Poland and we knew we were off and running with six points in the bank and a trip to Georgia on the horizon.

I had already been out to Georgia to take a look at the facilities and had decided that the best place for us to train would be in a dilapidated stadium away from the ground where we were due to actually play the match. The reason I picked it was because the pitch was better than a lot of other places on offer, one of them even had cowpats all over the field! On the morning after we arrived in Georgia for the match, I went with Glenn Roeder, who was also part of the coaching set-up, to take a look at the training pitch I'd decided on during my fact finding trip. When we got there we saw a guy juggling a football on the running track that surrounded the playing field. When Roeds and I went back with the team he was still there juggling with the football, and he continued to do it right through our training session. He never stopped, it was an amazing sight. One of the other things that sticks in my mind about that trip was the attitude of Stuart Pearce. He was left out of the team to play Georgia, but he was the perfect professional. Not a moan, not a grumble, but instead he trained brilliantly and was full of support and encouragement for the rest of the lads. Pearcey was a magnificent player and an example to any youngster. If he was in the squad you knew you could rely on him 100 per cent.

The team put in another great performance, with Teddy and Les Ferdinand scoring the goals. Gazza had a blinding game and David Batty was magnificent in a holding role. So with three games gone we'd managed to take maximum points, it was a tremendous way to start the campaign, but we also knew that we were about to face our toughest test so far with a game against Italy at Wembley.

We knew it would be a close match and so it proved to be, but results are everything when it comes to qualifying for a World Cup tournament and a goal from little Gianfranco Zola after 18 minutes was enough to separate the two sides and earn Italy a win. It was the first major set-back we'd had and it came in our biggest game so far. I soon realised just what an effect a defeat like that can have when it comes to the media. The press want England to win just as much as any fans, but there never really seems to be any middle ground when it comes to international football. A win has everyone on cloud nine and a defeat sends the country plummeting into a depression. Understandably the defeat did not go down well, but straight after the game Glenn was in a very positive frame of mind and was convinced we would not only qualify but do it as group winners.

Although I was the one who got all the publicity I wasn't the only Scotsman in the England camp. We used to have all of our training sessions and matches videoed and the man who did all the filming for us was Gary Guyan, a fellow Scot who did a great job supplying tapes that we would look at and analyse. For the training sessions Gary would set up his camera at a decent height so that we could get a better picture of what went on and how the players had looked. When it came to matches at Wembley he would be asked to go right to the top of the stadium to do his filming, and we would get a bird's eye view of all the action. This was particularly useful when it came to looking at the game against Italy and the way they had scored their goal.

"Look at that," Glenn said to me as we watched a tape of the Italy game in his office. "That's where we went wrong. We can't ever let that happen again."

We were able to see exactly what had happened when Zola scored his goal.

John Gorman

Our three centre-halves had left Italy's Casiraghi and Zola. They were in spaces and made the most of the room they'd been given. Seeing the tape only reinforced our view that we could do a lot better next time around.

"We'll learn from it and come back a lot stronger because of it," insisted Glenn.

Lots of people seemed to think we wouldn't be able to qualify after that Italy game, it seemed to have an instant effect with doubts creeping in, but Glenn had total belief that we would win through to the finals. We bounced back two months later with a 2-0 home win against Georgia, with goals from Teddy and Alan Shearer, and then produced a tremendous tactical display to beat the Poles 2-0 in Katowice. In preparation for the game we played a friendly against South Africa at Old Trafford, and the whole time we worked on the sort of tactic we would employ against Poland, trying to break with power and accuracy. We beat South Africa 2-1, but there was a downside to it all because we lost Jamie Redknapp with a broken ankle. It was a blow because Jamie was a lovely lad and a smashing player. When that sort of thing happens it's horrible, not just for the player but also for his family, and I remember trying to offer a few words of comfort to his dad Harry and the rest of the family after the game. The Poland match came at the end of May 1997. We had two qualifying games left to play. One would be against Moldova at Wembley in September and the other would be in Rome against Italy a month later.

Meanwhile, during the summer we took part in Le Tournoi playing matches against the hosts France, Italy and Brazil. We saw it as ideal preparation not only for the qualifying games, but also for the finals themselves which were going to be held in France a year later. It gave us all the chance of a 'dry run' and we were able to look at various facilities and get a taste of the sort of atmosphere we could expect. It was a very successful exercise because we won the tournament, beating Italy and France to make sure of the trophy, before losing our final game against Brazil in Paris.

It was nice to win the tournament, but we all knew the really important business was still about to take place. Paul Gascoigne produced a magnificent display to inspire the team against Moldova and we ran out comfortable 4-0 winners. Gazza got one of the goals, with Paul Scholes opening the scoring and Wrighty getting the other two. We also got an added bonus that night, because Italy drew 0-0 in their match in Georgia, meaning that we only needed a point in our final game to ensure qualification.

We knew that everything had to be spot on for our trip to Italy. There was so much riding on the match and we had to get it right both on and off the pitch. We used a training facility called La Borghesiana that was familiar to Gazza because he'd been there with Lazio. It was perfect for what we needed and the atmosphere in the camp was magnificent from the very first day. We were all very positive and determined to do the job, the preparation and training went really well and there was a buzz about the whole camp as we set off for the Olympic Stadium. We played a couple of videos on the team bus going to the game, one recalling past glories for England and the other showing the lads clips of themselves in action. We knew we had a great group of players and we wanted to let them see on film what they had done in the past. When the time came for us to go out on the pitch and warm the players up, I decided it would be a good idea to take them to the end where all the England supporters were gathered, so that the players could feed off the atmosphere the fans had already created.

The atmosphere in the dressing room was pretty special as well. It was relaxed without being too laid back and I got Wrighty going by playing a juggling contest with him as we waited to get the call to go on the pitch for the match. The game itself was one of the best I've ever been involved with, because of the disciplined and professional way we went about our business that night. There was belief running right through the side and the performance was magnificent. Glenn had decided to make Paul Ince captain and he absolutely revelled in the role. Incey is a true leader and as hard as they come. He had to go off in the first half to have stitches put in his head following a clash with Demetrio Albertini, but came back bandaged and raring to go. We knew that a draw would be enough but at one stage it looked as though we might win the game when Ian Wright came within inches of scoring, but instead hit the post. It was a heart-stopping moment for all of us on the bench, but we hardly had time to bemoan our luck because within seconds Christian Vieri almost scored for the Italians only to see his header go just wide. The strange thing was that as I glimpsed David Seaman in our goal, I could see that he seemed confident it was going wide, and after the game he told us just that. When the final whistle blew and we'd earned a 0-0 draw the coaching staff on the England bench were delirious. Ray Clemence, who was the goalkeeping coach, gave me a massive hug and then we grabbed hold of Glenn. We'd done what we'd set out to do. England were going to the World Cup Finals in France.

To be part of such a great occasion was a fantastic experience and one of the highlights of my career. Glenn's tactics had been absolutely spot on the team had performed brilliantly, I knew he must have been pleased and proud, but at the same time I also had a feeling there was something eating away at him, and very soon after that marvellous night in Rome I was to find out exactly what it was.

CHAPTER 11

WORLD CUP FEVER

When you've known someone for a long time it's not difficult to tell when something isn't quite right with them, and that's exactly how it was with Glenn. I'd thought for some time that there was something else on Glenn's mind that was deeper than football.

It never interfered with the way he went about his job, but something wasn't quite right. He must have sensed what I was thinking because he actually said he had something on his mind that I needed to know about, but with the Italy game occupying most of our thoughts at the time, we never really got around to having a chat. Even on the plane home after the game and in the car which picked us up, we never spoke about anything other than the match. We were also both exhausted from what had gone on in Rome.

What I didn't realise at the time was that within 24 hours of returning from

John Gorman

Italy Glenn told his wife Anne and their children that he was leaving. I just had a feeling something was wrong and I even mentioned it to Myra. Both of them were great friends and they had three wonderful kids, Zoe, Zara and Jamie, but from what Glenn later told me, their 18 years of marriage just came to an end.

The FA issued a statement on Glenn's behalf saying that, "with great sadness he has separated from his wife Anne," and that, "both Anne and Glenn would request that the privacy of themselves and of their children is respected at this very difficult and painful time." Of course, any hope of that happening went out of the window pretty quickly with both Glenn and Anne hounded by the media. He stayed with Myra and I for some of the time and also with other friends, but it wasn't a great time for him or for Anne and the kids. The end of a marriage should be a very private thing, but as manager of England you instantly seem to become public property and that extends to your family and friends as well. It's something you have to learn to cope with and come to terms with. Anyone who manages England has to be a pretty strong character and also be prepared to have their every move, both public and private scrutinised. You're in the spotlight from the day you agree to take the job, and I think that week Glenn experienced the good and the bad side of it. First there was the triumph in Italy and then there was the very public coverage of a very private matter.

Happily, not too long after the win against Italy we played a friendly against Cameroon at Wembley, winning 2-0 with goals from Paul Scholes and Robbie Fowler. It was also the game in which Rio Ferdinand made his debut, coming on as a substitute and looking really good. It was a great night for him and also for my neighbours and friends Richard and Paula. Richard was a West Ham fanatic and Rio was playing for the Hammers at the time. After the game

GORY TALES

Rio signed his shirt for Richard and he still has it hanging on his wall to this day. Being able to do little things like that were a great perk of the job I had, and it was always nice to be able to share some of the good times with friends and family.

By this time the focus was on who we would be playing in the World Cup Finals when we went to France. We'd already decided on where we would be staying for the tournament, having used the Hotel Du Golf near La Baule in northern France when we'd won Le Tournoi. It was a great place to stay with all the facilities we needed, and there was no problem getting to any of the locations that were going to be used for matches, because they were all within 90 minutes flying time.

The World Cup draw which was held in Marseilles was a huge event and it was suddenly apparent just how big being part of it all was going to be. England were paired with Romania, Colombia and Tunisia in Group G. From the moment the draw was made the real preparations for the tournament began. We had decided that part of the build-up for France would be a training trip to La Manga in Spain. That was also going to be where Glenn would make his decision on the squad that would be going to the finals. We played friendly matches, in February against Chile which we lost 2-0 and naturally got some stick because of the result. Then we went to Berne the following month and drew 1-1 with Switzerland, before beating Portugal 3-0 back at Wembley in April. It was all building nicely towards France and you could feel the excitement and expectation, there was also a lot of media attention that went with it all as well.

One of the stories to hit the headlines was the fact that Glenn had encouraged England players to see a healer called Eileen Drewery, and that she had been visiting the team hotel in the build-up to the Portugal match.

John Gorman

Eileen and her husband, Phil, were long-term friends of Glenn. He had first met her years ago when he was 18-years-old and had gone out with her daughter Michelle. Eileen had helped Glenn with a hamstring injury he had at the time and over the years he had gone to her with various injury problems. I went along to Eileen when I had all the trouble with my knee when I was at Spurs. Glenn suggested I see her, but I think I was probably too far gone and she wasn't able to really help me. What I do know is that quite a few of the England players had used Eileen and been very happy with what she had been able to do for them. As far as I'm concerned there's nothing wrong with any player seeking help with an injury, whatever form that help takes, and I can tell you from personal experience that having a bad injury is a terribly difficult thing to have to cope with. If Eileen can help players then what's the problem with that? It's all down to personal choice and belief in what is right for you, and it was well known that players like Paul Merson and Gazza had already seen her. As I've mentioned before, anything to do with the England team, its players and the staff is always going to make news, but from my own point of view all I wanted was to stay focused on the football and do my job.

Our last game in England before going to the World Cup was a friendly against Saudi Arabia at Wembley. It certainly wasn't a classic but the fans gave us a great send-off and once the match was over we were able to start thinking fully about the squad and the vital few weeks before the finals. A squad of 30 was named for the Saudi game and also two matches in the King Hassan II tournament in Casablanca against Morocco and Belgium. We flew to our base at La Manga a few days after the Saudi game. It was a perfect place to train and relax, with excellent facilities, which was why we were going to stay there and fly to the games in Casablanca, rather than stay in Morocco itself. La Manga was also going to be where the final squad for France would be announced, which meant there were going to be some very disappointed players.

We played the game against Morocco on 27th May, which also happened to be Gazza's 31st birthday, and won the match 1-0 with Michael Owen scoring a great goal. The sad news was that Ian Wright picked up a hamstring injury which was bad enough to put him out of the World Cup.

Poor Wrighty had already been battling with a groin problem and it was a real blow for him and the squad. He was a fantastic lad who was great to have around and there is no doubt at all, that he would have been in the squad had he remained fit. Ian was passionate about England and loved playing for his country. He was always a pleasure to have around on the training pitch and always gave everything in matches. He took the bad news well enough and put a brave face on things, but I knew how much it must have been hurting him inside, and I'm sure I saw a tear in his eye when I said goodbye to him before he flew back to London.

We flew to Casablanca for the Belgium game two days after playing Morocco, and everything seemed fine as the team bus left our hotel and headed for the airport, before someone suddenly shouted, "Where's Gazza?" Somehow we'd managed to leave without him. I think he was late getting to the bus, and our team doctor, John Crane, who for years had had the responsibility of counting everyone on and off, somehow managed to miss the fact that Gazza wasn't with us. It wasn't the happiest of games for Paul, he had to come off after about five minutes of the second half with a dead leg and a cut on his head.

Glenn was due to fly off after the match to have a look at one of our group opponents, Columbia, who were playing Germany in Frankfurt, but there was

John Gorman

a Spanish air traffic controllers' strike. With Glenn due to announce who was going to be going to the World Cup Finals and who, from the original 30-man squad would be left out, I suddenly thought he might not make it back in time. Instead it was decided that I would go with Glenn Roeder to watch the match, while Glenn would head back to La Manga. The trouble was that I hadn't expected to be going to Germany, and didn't even have a suit with me. In the end I had to borrow a belt and pair of shoes from Glenn and a suit from our travel manager, Brian Scott!

The next night I got a phone call from Glenn basically saying that he had real doubts about taking Gazza to the Finals. Glenn had spent the evening talking to Ray Clemence and under-21 manager, Peter Taylor. I think they too had their doubts about whether Gazza would be up to the task. It wasn't just one thing, it was the fact that for some time we'd felt Gazza's fitness levels just weren't good enough. Glenn said he'd phone me in the morning if he'd changed his mind, but the call never came and by the time I got back to La Manga with Roeds, I knew that Gazza was going to be one of the unlucky ones. With Wrighty and Jamie already ruled out because of injury it meant that there were going to be six very disappointed players heading out of La Manga that day on a private plane that was going to fly them back to Birmingham.

There's no easy way to tell a player that he is not going to be part of a World Cup squad, but Glenn wanted to break the news to the players face to face and let them know his thinking behind the decision. He'd allocated five minutes with all the players whether they were in or out, and as they came up to see him they first came in to see me and Glenn Roeder who was with me. I'd already heard from a couple of the lads that Gazza had had a few drinks and they'd marked my card saying it might be a good idea if I had a word with him.

GORY TALES

I knew Gazza wasn't going to be the only disappointed player we would have to deal with that day. Goalkeeper Ian Walker, Phil Neville, Dion Dublin, Nicky Butt and Andy Hinchcliffe were also going to be told that they would miss out. It was a terrible shame for all of them. They were smashing lads and I could really feel for them. It was also very upsetting for Gary Neville once he found out that his brother wouldn't be going to France. Both Roeds and I tried to comfort them as they came out after seeing Glenn and it wasn't a pleasant business, but at the same time it was part of being a footballer at the highest level, and the decision on who is in and who is out is not taken lightly.

When Gazza came to my room before seeing Glenn he was staring at me, but almost at the same time he was looking at Roeds to see if there was any clue as to what might be about to happen. Gazza knew Roeds from when they were both players with Newcastle and Glenn had been a good friend to him over the years. I knew it must have been really difficult for him as well. Suddenly Gazza started to speak.

"I'm not in it am I. I'm not in it," he said. He kept trying to get us to say whether or not he was in the squad, but of course that was something we couldn't do. Instead I walked towards him and was going to put my hand on his shoulder when he shouted at me.

"Don't touch me," he warned, and from the look of him I could see he was getting really agitated. I went and banged on the door of the Royal Suite, which was where Glenn was seeing the players and interrupted the conversation he was having with Andy Hinchcliffe.

"Glenn," I said. "I think you'd better see Gazza now."

I went in with Gazza and at first he seemed very angry. It was clear he knew the score and was aware that he wasn't going to France. He kept saying he couldn't believe it, but then he seemed to calm down and was fine. At that point I decided it was best that I leave and let Glenn have his chat with him, but I'd hardly got back to my room when I heard all sorts of noise coming from next door. Both Roeds and I rushed in and helped to get Gazza out, and eventually a couple of the other lads helped us to get him away and look after him. I found out that Gazza had really lost it for a few seconds when he was with Glenn, kicking a chair and then lashing out at a lamp. How he managed to come out without injuring himself, I don't know. It wasn't a very pleasant episode for anyone involved, and the backlash to the decision was predictable. There was a lot of stick flying Glenn's way, but the fact of the matter was that nobody would have loved to have had Gazza at the World Cup more than him. We both loved the guy, he was a superb player who could always add something to a side, but that was if he was fit. A fit Gazza would have gone to the World Cup and that was the bottom line. Gazza wasn't fit enough.

I've been in touch with Gazza over the years since that time in La Manga, and have always got on well with him. He's such a genuine guy and he would do anything for anybody. We all know that in more recent years he's had problems and anyone who has ever known him will wish him well. I'd like to think that I'm a friend and I also hope that he enjoyed the times we had on the training pitch and with England squads. He was a brilliant footballer, and despite that bitter disappointment in 1998, nobody can ever dispute that.

As horrible as it was for Gazza, it has to be said that after the decision had been made it seemed to give the younger players the chance to become stronger personalities, and I think they blossomed in his absence. People like David Beckham and Paul Scholes took on a new mantle.

We came back from La Manga with everyone knowing who was going to be in the squad for France and with the chance to relax a little before travelling to La Baule in preparation for the finals. We all had time with our friends and family and on the Saturday evening before we actually left for France we went as a group to the West End of London to see the musical *Chicago*, and then went on for a meal at Christopher's restaurant. That night really brought home how important the World Cup was to the nation, because we were mobbed by well-wishers after coming out of the theatre.

We flew to France on the Tuesday after that night out, stopping off in Caen to play a behind closed doors practise match against the Second Division team which we won 1-0. It was useful for us to see the players in match action six days before our opener against Tunisia in Marseille, and it was good for the players who hadn't had a game for almost two weeks.

Glenn picked his side for the Tunisia game and decided that David Beckham would not be starting the match. I'm sure it was a surprise to Becks, but the ultimate decision is always with the manager and players have to accept things like that. Don't get me wrong, I know just how upsetting it can be to be left out. After all, I certainly wasn't pleased all those years ago when Keith Burkinshaw dropped me, but at the same time all players are resilient, they have to be. Becks knew that his chance would come again during the course of the tournament. A lot has been written and said about the way our camp functioned during the time we were in France. Some people have even suggested that David was left out of the side because he didn't play golf, which is absolute rubbish. Lots of the boys liked golf and certainly Glenn and the rest of the coaching staff liked the game, but there were players in the squad who didn't really play and that was fine with us. Sol Campbell actually went off shopping instead of playing golf on one occasion, and when Becks came and asked me if he could go and see Victoria, who was his girlfriend at that time, there was never going to be a problem. Glenn said it was fine and David went off to spend some time with her at a local golf club near La Boule. He once asked me if it would be alright to meet up with Victoria when the England squad had been staying at Burnham Beeches, and I said it would be alright. Contrary to what some people might like to believe, the England players weren't treated like schoolboys. They were adults who were athletes at the top of their profession and we always tried to treat them as such.

We also tried to provide the right environment for the players to relax in and as well as the golf course, there was also a fully equipped games room where the lads could unwind if they wanted to. When it came to playing golf we nearly gave chief executive, Graham Kelly, a heart attack when we asked him if the FA would stump up the money to pay for golf shoes for the players. Actually Graham was fine about it. He was probably still in a mellow mood following his personal triumph in Rome when we'd drawn with the Italians. He took part in a staff five-a-side game during that trip and scored a hat-trick. We even gave him the autographed ball we'd all been playing with and I don't think it left his side the whole time we were in Italy!

We got our campaign off to a great start by beating Tunisia 2-0 with a goal from Alan Shearer just before the break and another from Paul Scholes in the last minute of the game. It was just what you hope for and certainly set us up nicely for what was going to be a tricky encounter with Romania in Toulouse seven days later.

We went behind in that match just after the break, but then Michael Owen put us on level terms in the 83rd minute, just 10 minutes after coming on as a substitute for Teddy. We thought we were going to get at least a draw from the match until Dan Petrescu popped up in the dying seconds to give them the win. It was a blow, but that sort of thing is what being in a World Cup is all about. There are set-backs and it's how you respond to them that is the important thing. Happily we didn't have long to dwell on the defeat because we had to play Colombia in Lens four days later in our final group game.

Becks had come on as a first half substitute for Incey during the Romania game and Glenn decided to start him against the Colombians. Within half an hour of the game kicking off David had fully justified his selection scoring in the 30th minute to add to Darren Anderton's goal, which had given us the lead 10 minutes earlier. The match finished 2-0 which meant that we would be facing Argentina in St Etienne on the last day of June. It was a great feeling to have made it to the second round of the competition, but everyone was well aware that there was a great deal of work still to be done if we were going to reach the quarter-finals.

The day after the Colombian game was our 28th wedding anniversary and Myra had travelled over on Eurostar with some of the other wives and girlfriends to see the game and then stayed over. Amanda came down with Rick on a motorbike and Nick had also made it over to France with some of his friends. The FA bought flowers for Myra and I. It was a lovely moment and a great way to celebrate our anniversary.

Once again we only had four days before playing our next game, but the players recovered well and there was a very good feel to the camp as we prepared for the match. We all realised just how important it was and there was a determination to make sure we saw the job through. I always felt it was going to be an exciting game with so many good players on the park, but I could never have imagined just how pulsating it actually turned out to be. Within six minutes of the start Argentina were awarded a penalty which Batistuta converted. Four minutes later Alan Shearer had scored for us and six minutes after that England were in front. It was a breathtaking goal and it came from Michael Owen, who at the time was only 18-years-old. It was a wonderful strike as he outstripped the Argentine defence and then was cool and clinical enough to score. We might well have got a third after that when Paul Scholes had a good chance, but then had to suffer the disappointment of conceding on the stroke of half-time when Zanetti equalised for them. I had met Zanetti when I went to Milan to watch Incey, he was a nice lad and we got on well while I was there, but at that moment I was calling him all sorts of names under my breath from the touchline.

If the equaliser was a bitter blow then so was what happened soon after half-time when David Beckham was sent off. Diego Simeone whacked Becks and as David was lying on the floor he stuck a leg out and caught the Argentine. Simeone made the most of it and referee Kim Milton Nielsen produced a red card. It was one of those things. Becks shouldn't have stuck a foot out, but at the same time it looked no more than a yellow card offence. We were down to 10 men but played really well for the rest of the second half and for the period of extra-time, when the first team to score would have won the game under the golden goal rule.

In fact we all thought we had won the game before extra-time, when Sol Campbell put the ball in the back of the net, only for the effort to be ruled out, and then our hearts were in our mouths as Argentina almost grabbed a winner at the other end before a great tackle from Gary Neville retrieved the situation for us. It meant we all had to suffer the nerve-wracking experience of a penalty shoot-out. As I walked onto the pitch at the end of the 120 minutes, the referee came up to me.

"John, don't worry you're going to win," he told me as I walked past him.

I couldn't believe what he'd said, but at the same time hoped he was right. We certainly deserved to win, but like anyone else I knew that once it comes to penalties the outcome of a game can be a lottery. You need brave players on occasions like these, people who have the confidence to step up and take responsibility. Argentina were the first to take a spot-kick. Berti scored for them and Shearer scored for us. 1-1. Crespo missed giving us hope that we could take the lead, but then Incey missed with his kick and Veron put them ahead. Paul Merson stuck his shot away to level things, but Gallardo scored. It was 3-2 to them. Up stepped young Michael showing maturity beyond his years and levelled things. It was left to Ayala to put the Argentineans in front again, leaving David Batty to take our last kick. I will always remember what Batts said as he went up to take the penalty.

"I'll get the glory," he joked, then missed the kick. England were out of the World Cup.

John Gorman

CHAPTER 12

SINNERS TO SAINTS

Let me say right now that the attitude of David Batty that night was superb. First of all he was brave enough to step up and take the kick, and then when he missed the penalty he was totally professional about the way he handled the situation. Of course he was hurting inside, and of course he probably felt as though he'd let everyone down, but Batts was big enough and had a strong enough character to handle it all. His quip about getting the glory wasn't bravado, it was his way of trying to make the rest of us relax and feel confident in what was a really tense situation. David Batty was superb throughout the time I was involved with England, and I would have loved him to be the man who did get the glory for us, because nobody would have deserved it more.

As you can imagine, our dressing room was not the happiest of places to be after the game. We were all stunned and it was a pretty silent place as the

Argentinean team celebrated down the corridor. We thanked all the players and told them that they couldn't have done more. I went in after the game and put my arm around David Beckham, I also later went to see his family as well who were really nice people and were always friendly with my own family whenever they met at matches. I knew Becks must be feeling terrible having got sent off. It was a stupid incident and one that I'm sure he regretted. Who knows what might have happened if we could have kept 11 men on the field. We were certainly the better team, even after David got a red card. The sending off later triggered a real backlash against him, and he had to suffer some terrible abuse from fans around the country, but although nobody should have to go through something like that just because of a football match, I'm sure it made him a stronger person and everyone knows that his career really blossomed after the World Cup. He was still just 23-years-old when he got his marching orders and it was a bitter lesson to learn. David was a shy lad when he first broke into the England side who worked really hard in training. It was obvious that he had a special talent and as the years have gone by he has become one of the game's superstars. He's certainly matured since that incident with Simeone and some of his performances, both for club and for country, have been outstanding. Happily, with all the fame and fortune he's had, I don't think he's changed too much, it would be a shame if he did. Basically he's still a lad who is happiest when he's kicking a ball around.

All the boys needed picking up not just because we'd lost but because of the way we'd lost. No team likes to go out of a competition on penalties and when he was asked after the game whether we'd practised taking them before the match David Batty said we hadn't. Being the honest lad that he is, Batts told the truth. We hadn't taken penalty kicks before the game because Glenn

John Gorman

wanted everyone to stay positive and not think about the game having to be decided in that way. The other point to make is that although we didn't practise penalties before the Argentina game, we had been taking them in training throughout the tournament, even varying them by taking the kick closer to the goal or further away. I also think it's impossible to replicate the sort of atmosphere and tension there is in a real penalty shoot-out situation. When they really happen it's all down to individuals and there's also quite a lot of luck involved.

The match against Argentina had been draining and I don't think I've ever been involved in a game that has been so exciting and tense. It was bad enough losing out, but what happened after the game left a bitter taste, when the Argentinean team taunted us from their team bus. The bus was rocking as they jumped about and shouted with their shirts off, not just in front of us but also our families and friends who had gathered outside the stadium. One of the worst offenders was Hernan Crespo, and you can only hope that in later years when he earned his living from playing with Chelsea, he might have come to regret trying to taunt the England team.

When the dust had settled a little and we'd all had time to reflect I believe we felt we went out of the competition earlier than we should have. Personally I think that the England team would have won the World Cup had we not slipped up against Argentina. The team had the capability and we had a great manager. Glenn had been so confident that we were going to go all the way and I totally agreed with him.

We didn't waste too much time hanging about in France following the game, and flew back the next day on Concorde, which was probably the shortest flight the plane had ever made. We got a great reception when we returned and I think people felt we had done all we could and that it was a cruel way to go out of the competition. I may have been a proud Scotsman, but it had been a privilege for me to be part of England's World Cup campaign and be associated with some great people. Not just the players but all the staff who had worked so hard. I thought back to that Brazil v Scotland match I'd been to eight years earlier and how great it had been just to watch the game and soak up the atmosphere. Being part of England's bid to win the World Cup in France was a special experience which I will never forget and my only regret is that we didn't go all the way.

I did go to the Final in Paris and watched France beat Brazil 3-0. I'd be lying if I said I didn't think of what might have been, but at least it proved to be a profitable trip. I was asked to do some corporate hospitality work and did a little talk about football to some invited guests during a cruise down the Seine on the way to the game. It was a nice way to end the World Cup, but I would have preferred to be on one of the touchline benches with England rather than watching everything unfold from the stand.

It was only 13 days since our exit against Argentina and I knew that in less than seven weeks time England would be in action against Sweden at the start of the Euro 2000 campaign. Things move on in football and it was going to be important to get over the World Cup disappointment and concentrate fully on the next big task, but before that it was time for Myra and I to have a good holiday. We'd made plans to travel to America for three weeks and visit old friends and my nephew who lived in the States, it was a trip both of us were really looking forward to.

At about four in the morning on the day we were due to travel to the USA Myra suddenly sat bolt upright in bed. It obviously woke me up and I could tell she seemed upset. She told me something had made her wake up and then said she could feel a lump in her breast. I'd been feeling sleepy but that news instantly brought me to my senses. Myra was understandably worried and asked me to feel the lump, it was obvious there was something wrong, but there was little we could do so early in the morning. We just had to wait and I told her that I would get on the phone at breakfast time and speak to Doc Crane. When I called him he could tell I was really concerned and also knew that we were due to fly to the States later that day.

"John, nothing much is going to change in three weeks," he told me. "Go and have your holiday and as soon as you come back I'll have things arranged for Myra to go and see a specialist."

We went to America and made the most of the trip, even though the lump and what it might mean was always at the back of our minds. We both tried to stay positive about the situation but there was no denying the fact that we were worried and it was obviously worse for Myra. She'd really been looking forward to the holiday and then had been knocked sideways by what had happened. Myra was very brave about it from the start, but there were the odd moments when she became tearful and started to think about what was going to happen. Doc Crane did exactly what he said he would and four days after arriving back in the country I went with Myra to see a specialist in London. It didn't take long to confirm what we had both feared. She had breast cancer.

I suppose we were both in shock really, even though we had suspected that was what it could be. The trouble is, until you get confirmation there is always the hope that it might be something else. When it dawns on you that your wife has cancer you suddenly feel very helpless, knowing that everything is out of your control. You begin to rely on the medical people and take encouragement from them when they tell you that this thing is beatable and it certainly isn't the end of the world, but at the same time I'd be lying if I said that it wasn't a very scary experience. I was the lucky one. It was poor Myra who had to deal not only with the physical side of things, but also the mental torture that I'm sure she went through. We also had to tell the kids. Amanda was working in the West End of London at the time and cycled over to meet us at the hospital after Myra had been diagnosed. It was upsetting for her and for Nick. We have always been a very close family and when kids hear news like that it is a very shocking experience, but at the same time we were all determined to help Myra with her battle.

The first stage was for her to have an operation five days later to actually remove the lump and then it was a case of having to undergo treatment involving chemotherapy and radiotherapy which would go on for a period of months. It wasn't going to be pleasant, but Myra was determined to beat the cancer and despite all that was happening, she somehow managed to remain remarkably upbeat. Ironically, my old friend Tommy Cannon knew exactly what we were going through, because his wife, Margaret, had also had breast cancer and was doing well after surgery and treatment. Glenn and the FA were really supportive and gave me as much time as I needed to go along with her when she had her treatment. One of the good things about the job I had with England was that it didn't have the day-to-day involvement of having to coach players as you would have with a club job. I was grateful for having more time with Myra and tried to make the most of it, but the fact was that two weeks after she had her operation, I had to get ready to travel with the England squad for our first Euro 2000 qualifier away to Sweden in Stockholm. I knew that in a professional sense it had to be business as usual, and I needed to get on and do my job, but I was also aware that I was leaving Myra in the build-up to the game and would then be out of the country for a few days, just as she was recovering from her operation and undergoing her treatment. I knew there were family and friends who would be there for her, but it probably wasn't the best of times for me to be involved in such a crucial game. If I'm being selfish I have to say that getting stuck into the work and being out on a training pitch with players probably helped me, but the result we got out there certainly wasn't much of a tonic.

After getting a great start with a goal from Alan Shearer after just 75 seconds, we conceded two in two minutes during the first half and also had Paul Ince sent off. When Incey walked off he got some stick and seemed to gesture at the crowd, after the game he told the media that he'd been having a go at me and so that's what everyone thought. Paul spoke to me afterwards and said that although he'd told them that, he'd actually lost it a bit with the crowd, so I became the fall guy for him. To be honest I didn't really mind. I liked Paul a lot but he had a bit of a fiery temper and I knew it had all been done in the heat of the moment. Like everyone else connected with the England team that night he was disappointed and frustrated.

Predictably the knives soon started to come out and we knew that there was pressure on us. Glenn had already got some stick the month before for bringing out a book about the World Cup, which he'd written with the help of the FA's public affairs director, David Davies, and when the result in Sweden went against us I felt there was a definite change in the media and perhaps amongst some fans. The next month we played the second match in our qualifying group, but could only manage a goalless draw at Wembley against Bulgaria. The reaction was understandably bad, but at least we had the chance to put the result behind us pretty quickly when we went to Luxembourg four days later and gained our first win in the group with a 3-0 victory. It wasn't a great performance and much was made of the fact that our opponents had part-time players in their side, but no game at international level is easy, and at least we'd put a win on the board.

People always like to talk about the pressure involved in football, and of course, like any other job it does have its moments of stress. Those moments are probably a lot bigger when you're talking about the England team because, as I've said, everything you do as a manager or coach is big news. When things are not going well, there are more than enough people willing to tell you you're not doing your job properly and also how it could be done better. I've always tried to be frank and open with the press. Over the years I've made some good friends with people in the media and I've always recognised that they have a job to do. One day I was giving an interview to a reporter who asked me all about the pressure of the job.

"There's not that much pressure, when you compare it to your wife having cancer," I told him.

I could see his eyes widen after I said it and he obviously knew he had a bigger story on his hands than he'd imagined. In the end he did a very nice sympathetic piece about Myra's illness. The only trouble was that by the time it had been picked up by some papers in Scotland the story had changed a bit, and when Myra's family read about it they thought she'd had her breasts removed, which wasn't the case.

She continued to have treatment towards the end of 1998 and we got a lot of encouragement from the doctors and staff who were looking after her. It was all positive news as the year came to an end. As far as England was concerned we knew we would face another huge game at the end of March 1999 when Poland were due to visit Wembley in another qualifying game. There can often be big gaps in between international matches, which can sometimes be a problem for coaches and managers. It's not just that you won't have a chance to work with players for a long time, it's also that you're only as good as your last performance. In our case the result had been good, but the performance had been criticised, and that is always likely to stick in people's minds.

As the New Year started Glenn and I were focused on preparing for the Poland game and although performances had not been great since returning from the World Cup, I think we both felt that the tide would turn and that we could certainly qualify for Euro 2000. There had been criticism but I still thought Glenn's job was safe and that he'd be able to ride out any storms on the playing front. Unfortunately what hit him was more like a hurricane and it had nothing to do with football.

At the end of January Glenn did an interview with Matt Dickinson from *The Times*, in which he talked about his beliefs. As part of the interview Glenn spoke about people with disabilities. His comments caused uproar.

I don't want to get into what was said and what wasn't said by Glenn, all I do know is that to even suggest that he did not like or care about disabled people is total and utter rubbish. Anyone who knows him will realise what a caring and compassionate human being he is. Of course he has his faults, we all do, but some of the things that were written and said after that article was published were absolutely horrible and a disgrace.

Within a matter of days after the article was published Glenn lost his job. On the day he left Glenn phoned me and said that he thought something was going to happen. He went into a meeting with the FA and told me that he would phone to let me know the outcome. I sat in my car for ages in the middle of Hyde Park, just around the corner from where he was having his meeting, waiting for my mobile to ring. When it did Glenn told me he was leaving and that I'd better come over and try to sort out my own situation with the FA, which was what I did. I'd expected them to want me to go along with Glenn, but instead they asked me to stay on. They also wanted me to help the FA's technical director, Howard Wilkinson, to prepare the England team for their friendly game at Wembley against World champions France in eight days time. Glenn told me he had no problem with me staying on and I was happy to help Howard, but I also knew that I didn't really see things the same way as him when it came to playing football. We got on fine, but I didn't feel we were on the same wavelength and the French ran out comfortable winners when we played them.

It was all very strange for me because I didn't feel the same, there was also talk of Kevin Keegan coming in to take over as manager, and I knew that he would probably want his own people with him. I made the decision that it would be best for me to go and virtually said as much to the FA. We came to an agreement and I have no problems with them at all. I was treated well during my time working for the Football Association, and as well as getting to work with some fantastic players and coaching staff, I also loved every minute of my time working with some wonderful people away from the training pitch, like our international administration assistant, Michelle Farrer, who did so much to help make things run smoothly for Glenn and I.

It was a sad day when I said goodbye to her and to all the other staff. It was a shame because I think Glenn could have been one hell of an England manager, being his assistant was quite possibly the best job I ever had and certainly one of the highlights of my career. Probably the hardest thing for me was being Scottish. Lots of Scots couldn't understand how I could work as part of the England set-up. Perhaps it was because it hadn't ever happened before and attitudes were different. As far as I was concerned it was a great job, and I'll always be sad that it came to an end in the way it did.

From the very first day we were married Myra always worried about the

John Gorman

future. Now with me out of work and her still receiving treatment I knew she would be concerned. The last thing I wanted was for her to have more worries on top of all she had gone through. I was always conscious that I had to work. We had our house and a bit saved up, but nothing that was going to allow me to be out of work for long, so when I got a call from George Burley asking me if I'd consider going to work as first team coach for him at Ipswich, I didn't need much persuading to say yes. George liked his team to play good, attractive football and although Ipswich was quite a way from my home in Berkshire, I was pleased to be employed again. The money Ipswich offered me was almost the same as I had been getting as Glenn's assistant with England. Contrary to what a lot of people might have thought I didn't earn fantastic money during the time I had the England job, and neither did Glenn or Terry Venables before him, but the job itself was fantastic and I always found the FA good people to work for.

There was a great spirit at Ipswich and the team were going well when I arrived, challenging for a promotion place from Division One. George was a strong and honest character, who enjoyed doing a lot of the training himself. It meant that I wasn't doing as much coaching as I'd been used to in the past, but the job itself was good. I would travel up, leaving at about 5am and maybe stay over a couple of days a week, but I was also able to get home for much of the week, although it involved a lot of travelling.

The team did well and finished third in the table, just missing out on automatic promotion. It meant that we had to try and get promotion via the play-offs, meeting Bolton in a two leg semi-final. We lost the first leg by the only goal of the game and then beat them 4-3 at home, but at that time the away goal rule applied and although the aggregate score was 4-4, Bolton got through to the Wembley final because they had scored three times at our place. It was a cruel way to miss out on possible promotion, particularly for George who had experienced being knocked out at the same stage the year before by Charlton. I had only been part of the effort towards the end of the season, but early in the summer Ipswich offered me a two year contract with them, so they must have thought I did a decent job for them. It was a tempting offer and the money was very decent, but at the same time it was a long way from my home and I thought it might be best to have a bit of a break and take stock.

Myra later told me that she was disappointed I'd taken the Ipswich job so soon after leaving England. She wished we could have spent a bit more time together, and although I said yes to the job for what I thought were the right reasons, I have to say that I now regret I didn't spend more time with her. The initial treatment had ended, but it was still very early days and I should have been with her more. I also have to admit I found her having cancer difficult to handle. It wasn't that I didn't care it was more a case of wanting to stay busy and be upbeat. We were both very positive about everything and she was brilliant in the way she just tried to carry on as normal. I never really had any thoughts about another job after leaving Ipswich and Myra and I both decided that we would see what came along. The one thing I didn't really want to do was commit myself to any sort of long-term contract at that point, but at the same time I knew I had to work. I felt it had to be something that would fit in with what was happening with her at that time.

As the pre-season training period began I got a call from Denis Smith who was managing West Bromwich Albion. I'd known Denis for some time and we often used to talk when I was at Swindon and he was the boss at Oxford. He invited Myra and I up for a chat and said that he'd like me to join him as a coach, but there was no contract involved, I would just get a monthly salary.

John Gorman

It seemed like a really good offer and the nice thing was that Myra was pleased with it as well. Most of the time I could commute, because the drive wasn't that bad, and when I did have to stay over Denis said I could stay with him in his apartment.

I soon got stuck into the pre-season training and Denis was quite happy for me to do most of it, which really suited me. We went and played a couple of games on tour and then came back to prepare for another friendly at Albion's ground, The Hawthorns. On the day before the game after training John Wile, the chief executive, pulled me to one side and told me that the board had just relieved Denis of his duties. They put me in temporary charge and then suggested that I throw my hat into the ring when it came to them choosing a new manager. Denis was fine with the idea of me putting my name forward, but before I knew what had happened, Brian Little had been installed as the new boss, and was more than happy to have me alongside him as coach. I'd only been there five minutes, the season hadn't even started, and I was already on my second manager!

I got on really well with Brian and the team were unbeaten in their first nine league games. Denis had said that I could use his apartment if ever I wanted to stay overnight, and one day I was on my way there when my mobile phone rang. It was my old mate Keith Peacock, who was assistant manager of Charlton at the time. He wanted to know if I would be interested in a job, not at Charlton, but at Reading. He told me that Alan Pardew was in with a chance of getting the manager's job there, but that he probably needed someone with experience alongside him. Would I be interested?

Reading was virtually on my doorstep and Nick was already working there as part of their Football in the Community set-up. Although I was really enjoying my time at WBA, the whole idea of working closer to home immediately had an appeal, especially after what had happened with Myra. I agreed to go along with Pards to meet the Reading chairman John Madejski. We got the job and immediately began work on trying to get them up the league.

They were already in a bit of a battle at the bottom, and it was hard going. I liked the actual job and got on fine with Pards, but I was never really able to win over the fans. As far as they were concerned I was just the ex-manager of Swindon, who are one of their relatively local rivals. It was a shame, because there was a great set-up with a lovely new stadium, but it never quite felt right although I was prepared to stick at it because I always thought things would turn around on the playing side. It was amazing really because I'd worked for three clubs since leaving the England job less than a year earlier. I certainly hadn't planned it that way but sometimes these sort of things happen, and early in the New Year I got the chance to move on yet again.

Glenn phoned me one day and said that there was a very good chance he could soon be back in management, and that he'd like me to go with him. "Here we go again!" I thought as I put the phone down. Not long after we were in talks with Southampton, with Glenn taking over as manager on an initial 12 month contract from Dave Jones.

It was almost a year since Glenn had left the England job, and he was clearly in the mood to get back to management once more. I was happy to be working with him again and it was obviously good for me to get the chance of being with a club who were in the Premiership. Although I hadn't been at Reading for very long, there was never a problem with me leaving. I already had an agreement with them that I could leave if a Premiership side came in for me, so I was able to shake hands with Alan and the chairman and left on good terms. I'm really pleased Reading went from strength to strength and

John Gorman

still get a very warm welcome from all the people there whenever I go back.

I've been very lucky in my career to have worked with some great people at some smashing clubs. That was certainly true of my time with Southampton, with both Glenn and I settling in really quickly. It wasn't a big club but the chairman, Rupert Lowe, had big ambitions which included moving into a new stadium in the summer of 2001. I felt as if I was joining a club with an exciting future, but also one that had a really nice feel to it. The fans were good and although the Dell was a cramped little ground, it had tremendous atmosphere and teams certainly didn't like playing there.

Glenn and I often used to share the driving down to the club's Marchwood training ground, where for some reason or other it always seemed to be sunny. It was a good place to coach with very decent facilities and I got on well with Stuart Gray, who used to share the first team coaching with me. The two of us also used to spend a lot of time coaching some of the younger lads after the regular sessions had finished, people like Matt Oakley, and also Wayne Bridge who later went on to play for Chelsea and England. There was always a great atmosphere at the training ground and after we'd finished for the day, we'd get a net out and all the coaching staff, Glenn, me, Stuart and Dennis Rofe, would have a game of head tennis. We used to drive our poor secretary, Daphne, mad because we'd often start at about four in the afternoon and still be playing at six. Poor Daph was waiting to go home and the training ground still had to be locked up! It was also a happy time for my family. Nick used to love coming to the home games and so did Myra, who by this time was doing really well and seemed very contented with me working at Southampton.

There were some good players there, with the likes of Dean Richards, Kevin Beattie, Kevin Davies, and Matt Le Tissier in the squad. Of course we

GORY TALES

knew Matt from our England days and both Glenn and I thought he was an exceptional talent, even though he hadn't quite made it into the World Cup squad. He was already a Southampton legend, and rightly so, because he had probably rescued the club on the playing pitch almost single handed on so many occasions. He could make the ball talk and was technically one of the best players England has ever had. Glenn went overboard with Matt to try and get him right and help keep his career going. But he had injuries and his fitness suffered as a consequence. We certainly wanted a fit Matt Le Tissier in the team because he was a special player who could turn a game for you with one piece of magic from either foot. Unfortunately he didn't figure in the side as much as we would have liked him to.

We had 15 league games left when we took over that season, and ended up having a steady rather than spectacular end to the season, but the feeling during the summer was that we could start to push on during the course of the new season. We started pretty well and towards the end of September with seven league games played we found ourselves eighth in the table having put in some very good footballing performances. We continued to play well despite some mixed results which saw us slip down the table a little, but quite early in the New Year our results suddenly began to reflect our form and the good football we were playing.

After losing to Liverpool on New Year's Day, we went on a run which saw us draw two matches and then put together a five game winning streak which took us back to eighth in the table. It was a great feeling and with a gap in the league programme coming up because of international matches that were going to be played in March, Glenn and I both took the opportunity to get away for a short break. He went off to South Africa with his new wife Vanessa, while Myra and I went with our friends Richard and Paula Bury to La

John Gorman

Manga. Richard and I had been drawn to play golf against each other in a competition organised by one of our local pubs, but we were allowed to play the match on any course we wanted, so I suggested playing in La Manga and Richard didn't need too much persuading. It was nice to be able to go away and not worry about football. We'd had a great run and everything looked set for a rosy future. It had been a good 14 months, the club were happy with us and we were happy at the club. I was looking forward to getting back to Marchwood and training the players when I returned from La Manga. Everything seemed very settled, and then I got a phone call.

"John it's me," said Glenn. "You'll never guess what – I've been given permission by the chairman to speak to Tottenham."

CHAPTER 13

HOMECOMING

If it had been any other club I'm not sure Glenn would have gone. Despite a lot of the criticism we got at the time, we both really liked being at Southampton, and genuinely thought the club were moving in the right direction, but getting the chance to manage Tottenham was like a dream for Glenn.

You have to remember that not only was he one of the best players ever to have worn a Spurs shirt, but also that his whole family were Tottenham fanatics. He'd been brought up with Spurs in his blood and the pull of going back to White Hart Lane as the club's manager was just too much to resist. I'd only spent a relatively short time at Tottenham, but it was one of those places that have a lasting effect. I became a Spurs man. My son Nick was a Tottenham supporter and so was Amanda's boyfriend, Rick, so to go back

John Gorman

there as assistant manager was a wonderful opportunity for me as well.

When I came back from La Manga I went into the club to shake hands and say goodbye to everyone, including the chairman Rupert Lowe, who said he was disappointed I was going.

"You can't be that disappointed," I told him.

"Why?" he asked.

"Because you never asked me to stay!" I said.

When a similar situation had occurred at Swindon eight years earlier, the chairman had made it quite clear that they wanted me to stay on, but that was never the case at Southampton.

"We just assumed you'd be going with Glenn," Rupert claimed.

To be honest, there was never any real likelihood that I wouldn't go to Tottenham. As I've said, the pull of going back to White Hart Lane was just too strong, but I was never actually asked to stay on by Southampton. Glenn and I met the Tottenham chairman, Daniel Levy and David Buchler, who was the club's executive vice-chairman at the time. Both of them were desperate for the good times to return for Spurs, and were clearly delighted to have got Glenn back to the club as its manager. The fans loved it as well. Many of them still remembered him from his playing days and those who hadn't actually seen him were still aware that he was a true Tottenham legend.

Glenn took over from George Graham who had been in charge for just over two years and had led Spurs to a Worthington Cup Final win in 1999. He had also managed to get the side we inherited into the FA Cup semi-final. That was the good news. The bad news was that it was against Arsenal, who had become a real force under Arsene Wenger. They had finished runners-up in the Premiership the season before and at the time were second in the table. Glenn and I officially took over at Tottenham on 30 March 2001, and the next day the two of us sat in the Highbury stands as Arsenal beat Tottenham 2-0 in a league match that marked Arsene's 250th game in charge of the Gunners. It was also a dress rehearsal for what would be our first game at the helm with Spurs, the semi-final that was due to take place a week later at Old Trafford.

I can't say the FA Cup held many happy memories for us that season, because while we were at Southampton only seven weeks earlier we'd gone to Tranmere for a fifth round replay having drawn at home 0-0. We looked as though we were going to ease home in the replay when we took a 3-0 lead in the first half, but after the break we were on the wrong end of one of the biggest turnarounds in the Cup, and ended up losing the game 4-3, which was a devastating blow.

We knew that trying to get the better of Arsenal at any time was a difficult task, but just to add to our problems in the build-up to the semi-final, we had to contend with lots of injuries, including a big doubt about whether Sol Campbell would make it. We stayed at Mottram Hall and on the morning of the game I gave Sol a fitness test in the grounds of the hotel. He was able to do all that I asked of him, but at the same time I knew he wasn't 100 per cent fit. We needed him to play because he was such a big presence in the side and a great leader. Sol had been part of Tottenham for a long time and we knew from our England days just what a good player he was. We also knew that whatever happened against Arsenal, there was a very good chance that we would lose him altogether, because he seemed destined to leave the club on a free transfer.

Sol did his best for us that day and so did the rest of the lads. The Tottenham fans gave Glenn and I a great reception and when we took the lead through Gary Doherty after 14 minutes it looked good for us, but Patrick

John Gorman

Vieira equalised before the break and Robert Pires scored the winner in the second half. It was a really good effort from the boys but no defeat against Arsenal goes down well with Spurs fans and we knew that a lot would be expected of us in the weeks and months ahead as Tottenham tried to challenge the dominance the Gunners had enjoyed in recent years.

We had a chance to look at the squad and assess things in the seven games left before the end of the season, and knew there was work to be done, but the prospect was exciting and there was definitely a wave of optimism about the place because Glenn had returned. That optimism was reinforced during our last game of the season when we had a 3-1 win against champions Manchester United at White Hart Lane, and there was a lot of expectation for the start of our first full season in charge.

We brought some experience into the squad during the summer of 2001, with the arrival of Teddy Sheringham from Manchester United, Gus Poyet from Chelsea and Cristian Ziege from Liverpool, but Glenn could do nothing to stop what had become the inevitable when Sol eventually went early in July. The real shock wasn't so much the fact that he left, but it was where he went to that really upset Spurs fans when he signed for Arsenal. We thought he might go abroad because there were apparently quite a few of the top European sides willing to sign him, but at the age of almost 27, and with nine first team seasons behind him at Tottenham, he decided to switch to the club's biggest rivals, which obviously didn't go down too well. Chris Hughton used to share the first team coaching duties with me, and he was very close to Sol. I know he tried to persuade him to stay as well but he was determined to go and I think he had been for some time before we arrived.

Although it was disappointing to lose him, there's no way you can blame a player for making a decision that he feels will benefit his career. Sol went to a team where he started winning things from day one and he was very well paid for doing it. Good luck to him. He's a lovely lad and a class performer, it was just a shame we couldn't have had just one more season from him, because I think it would have helped us and helped the club. These things happen and you have to move on, although it would be silly to pretend he wasn't a big loss to us.

We knew we had to get a quality defender in and Glenn turned to Southampton and big Dean Richards who had done so well for us when we were there. He came in the September and on the day after he signed I was even more delighted with another arrival. On 22 September Amanda gave birth to Aaron. I was a granddad and I couldn't have been happier. Myra was the birth mother helping our daughter bring the little guy into this world, as I paced up and down outside with Rick, the proud father. A week after Aaron was born we had a home league match with Manchester United and it looked as though I was going to be able to celebrate becoming a granddad in style, because we romped into a 3-0 half-time lead. If losing at Tranmere with Southampton was hard to take, what happened in the second half against United was even worse. They somehow managed to turn the game upside down and from looking like winners we ended up losing the match 5-3. United were exceptional that day, but it was very hard to take. The one thing that really helped cheer me up was the thought of little Aaron. It was a fantastic experience to have a grandson, and it wasn't too long before he made his first appearance at White Hart Lane. Amanda and Rick chose a great game for his first Spurs match, because it was the day Les Ferdinand scored the Premiership's 10,000th goal, when he netted in our 4-0 win against Fulham. Big Les signed a programme for Aaron with a special little message and it's something I know he will always treasure.

John Gorman

By the time Les scored that goal we were just outside the top six positions. We had also done well in the Worthington Cup, getting through to the semi-final stage where we met Chelsea over two legs early in the New Year. They were just above us in the Premiership, having made steady progress for the past few years and under manager Claudio Ranieri and were beginning to become a major force in the English game. We lost the first leg 2-1 at Stamford Bridge and I think a lot of people thought Chelsea would be too much for us in the second leg as well, but we produced a great performance scoring five times before Chelsea finally got a consolation goal in the last minute of the game. We were through to a final in our first full season in charge, there was genuine excitement at the club and we knew that a win could prove to be the sort of launch pad we were looking for. It would not only mean a trophy, it would also mean European football if we won, so the final against Blackburn at the Millennium Stadium in Cardiff on Sunday 24 February was going to be a huge game for us.

You always want your preparation for a big game to be spot on and that's what we tried to do in the week leading up to the Final. We were in really good spirits having done so well in the semi-final, and although we weren't over confident there was a very positive feel to everything we did. The game was being played on a Sunday, but on the Thursday before the match Myra received some terrible news, when she was told that her father, Lewis, had died.

Having got through all the problems and treatment connected with her cancer, to get news like that was a horrible blow, but once again she coped with it all really well. I think she was also conscious that I was involved in helping to prepare the team for the Final. It was a lot for her to have to cope with, but in typical Myra fashion, she did just that and made it to Cardiff three days later to watch us against Blackburn.

When the big game came we never did ourselves justice. After Matt Jansen put them in front Christian Ziege equalised for us, before Andy Cole got Blackburn's winner. It was a real disappointment and everyone felt flat, because there had been a lot of expectation before the game and we really thought we were going to win a trophy. It wasn't a nice feeling, but what had happened a few days before with Myra's father put the whole thing into perspective, and so did a tragedy suffered by Glenn a couple of days later.

We had the players in for their first training session since the final and were trying to give them a bit of a lift following all the disappointment of what had happened in Cardiff. I suddenly saw our secretary, Irene, walking onto one of the training pitches looking concerned. I knew something must be wrong and ran over to see what the problem was.

"John, it's Glenn's dad, he's been rushed to hospital," she told me. I could tell from her face that it must be serious, and sprinted over to tell Glenn. We drove to the hospital but within 24 hours his dad, Derek, had passed away. It was an awful shock for him and his family. Some people might think losing a cup final is a tragedy, believe me it isn't, but losing a parent is. It was almost unbelievable that both Glenn and Myra had experienced that loss within days of each other. Later that same year poor Myra also had to deal with the death of her mother Elsie, who died just nine months after her husband.

Our form for the rest of the season was indifferent and we seemed to slip away after losing to Blackburn. We had a good run in the FA Cup that season as well reaching the sixth round, but came unstuck at home to Chelsea who beat us 4-0. To make matters worse, Chelsea really made sure they got revenge for that semi-final defeat, when they repeated the score to take all three points off of us in a league game at Stamford Bridge. That defeat was one of three on the bounce for us and although we did pick up a bit in the remaining games we had, we ended the season in ninth position having lost our last match of the season, while West Ham won their final game and ended up in seventh place. It was disappointing, but at the same time the season certainly hadn't been a disaster. We'd reached a cup final, got to the quarter-finals in another competition and finished ninth in the Premiership, the highest the club had been in the league since 1996.

There was still plenty to feel optimistic about when the new season began and with one defeat in our first six league matches we found ourselves second in the table. We also signed a player who went on to become a huge favourite with everyone at Tottenham, when Robbie Keane arrived from Leeds at the end of August 2002. Robbie was a delight to be with on the training pitch. His attitude and skill was tremendous. He would always be looking to do extra stuff and never stopped working at his game. He's the sort of player Spurs fans love to watch and it's been great to see the way he has just got better and better.

Although we started well we slipped a little as the season went on but were never far away from the top six. We had a disappointing exit from the Worthington Cup when we were knocked out at Burnley in the third round and were then dealt a double blow by Southampton at the turn of the year. On New Year's Day we went to St Mary's stadium and lost by the only goal of the game in a league match, and then three days later returned to the South Coast only to be beaten 4-0 in the third round of the FA Cup. It was a terrible result, and even worse for Glenn and I because of our past connection with the club and the fact that we'd left to take over at Tottenham. We got some terrible stick from the Saints fans and just had to take it on the chin as the goals hit the back of the net.

GORY TALES

Despite that heavy defeat we still had realistic hopes of getting into Europe, but didn't have a good end to the season. In our last 11 matches we only managed two wins, against Birmingham and West Bromwich Albion, and lost seven games, including the last three of the season. There was talk in the press that we could be on our way out, despite the fact that the team had played some really good football that season. We finished 10th in the table but we knew that more was expected of us. We also felt when we arrived at Tottenham that things couldn't be done overnight, it was going to be a gradual process and we needed time to get it right. But as we all know, time is in short supply when it comes to trying to achieve success in football.

Glenn and I were called in for a meeting with the board. Daniel Levy and his fellow director, Paul Kemsley, genuinely wanted Glenn to do well. They were as desperate for success as we were and had always treated us well. It was nothing personal, as they say, but it was also clear after that meeting that if we didn't get a good start to the next season we could be on our way out of White Hart Lane.

CHAPTER 14

WHITE HART PAIN

The pressure was on but that's nothing new in football, and if you're going to be in charge of a club like Tottenham where the expectations are high then pressure comes with the job. Glenn knew that when he took over and so did I. We were confident that we could get a good start and then push on from there. At least that was the plan, but football has a habit of wrecking plans and in the Premiership there are no easy games.

We started the season with a 1-0 defeat at Birmingham, but then bounced back well with a 2-1 home win against Leeds before putting in a really good display to earn a goalless draw at Liverpool. Four points from a possible nine might not sound great, but the performance at Liverpool was encouraging and it was still very early days. However our next game produced a terrible result when we lost 3-0 at home to Fulham and then got beaten by their West

GORY TALES

London neighbours Chelsea 4-2 at Stamford Bridge. They were bad results and I knew we needed a big performance in our next game, which was at White Hart Lane against Southampton.

By this time Aaron had become quite a regular at home games, and would often sit with Amanda and Myra in the stand just behind the dug-out where the home bench was. Despite the fact that there were usually 36,000 people in the stadium, I would often hear his little voice calling out "granddad" behind me during quiet spells in the game. It could be quite disconcerting at times, because Glenn would be watching the game from the director's box and used to phone down to me when he wanted to talk about something happening in the game. So I'd have him on the phone and little Aaron trying desperately to get a wave from his granddad. On the day we played Southampton Aaron was up in the stand behind me and I remember waving to him as the game started. By half-time we were 2-0 down and I had a bad feeling about what was going to happen. We lost the match 3-1. A terrible result and our third in a row, it was ironic that it had to be against Southampton, and as I walked to the dressing room I couldn't help feeling that it might be our last game in charge of Tottenham. It was sad because it had been such an important match for us, but then I looked up into the stand to try and catch a glimpse of Aaron. Nobody likes the thought of losing their job, but when I saw his little face I realised it wasn't the end of the world if it did happen. He helped to remind me that there are more important things in life than football. I suppose I knew our jobs were on the line before the game and after it I had the same sort of feeling I had when I was at Swindon and we'd played Bristol City. I knew I was going to get the chop, and I thought it would be soon.

I said as much to Richard and Paula when I invited them round to share a bottle of wine with Myra and I the next day. It was a beautifully warm late

John Gorman

September afternoon and I suggested we all relax in the Jacuzzi I had in my garden. There didn't seem to be much point in moping about the result the previous day and the four of us were all sitting there having a drink and a laugh when I thought I heard the phone ringing. I let it ring a few times but then decided I ought to answer it before it stopped ringing, but I was too late. The message light was flashing and I pressed the replay button. The first message was from Daniel Levy, who I knew was on his honeymoon, so I realised it must be important. He said that he wanted me to contact Paul Kemsley because he had something to tell me, and that I should do it right away. The second was from Glenn basically saying that the inevitable had happened and that we were out of a job. Just as I was listening to the message, I heard Myra shout from the lounge.

"John you and Glenn have been sacked," she told me. "It's on teletext, and they've put David Pleat and Chrissy Hughton in charge."

David Pleat was the club's director of football and had been a Tottenham manager before. Chris was the first team coach and the club had acted quickly to put them in temporary charge. David was already director of football when we arrived and we worked with him throughout the time we were at Tottenham. He was never a problem to me and my relationship was fine with him. I always thought his knowledge of players, particularly young players was very good, and I think he'd helped to bring a lot of youngsters through. I suppose that in his position he always had to have two hats on. He had to deal with us and with the board. The director of football is a relatively new role in the English game, and not all clubs feel it's necessary to have someone in that position as well as a manager. As things turned out for the rest of that season, David ended up having to combine the two roles, with him acting as caretaker until a new manager was appointed as Spurs finished

14th in the Premiership.

Getting the news that Sunday afternoon brought a disappointing end to our time in charge and it was probably more so for Glenn. He'd taken the job with really high expectations and was desperate to do well because Spurs meant so much to him. It felt like a case of unfinished business for both of us. We knew the results had been disappointing, but we'd still only had six games of the season and when you looked at the fixtures that were coming along, I felt we were more than capable of picking up some points and climbing the table. It was barely two and a half years since we'd been appointed and to this day I still feel we could have turned things around had we stayed at the club. Don't get me wrong, we both knew that Daniel and the rest of the board wanted success and they wanted it quickly. I know they liked us and we liked them, which may sound strange considering they sacked us, but in the end they made a decision that they thought was right for the club. When I did phone Paul Kemsley on that Sunday he was genuinely upset that things hadn't worked out. I'm sure they would have loved Glenn to have had the success that we all wanted, but in the end he wasn't given the time and there certainly wasn't the sort of money around then that has been available at Tottenham in recent years. I don't feel bitter about what happened, just sad. I'm pleased to say I remain on good terms with the club and White Hart Lane will always be a special place for me. Although things didn't work out, I still enjoyed my time there and loved being out on the training pitch. I like to think that wherever I've been I've always had a good rapport with the players and Tottenham was no exception.

A few days later I went in to collect some personal belongings and say goodbye to the staff. It was a sad occasion for me but I had to chuckle when I walked in and saw Colin Calderwood, my old player from Swindon who we'd

John Gorman

brought in as reserve team manager, sitting in my chair.

"I've only been gone a couple of days and you've jumped into my seat!" I joked.

We all had a laugh about it but the truth was that in football your life can change overnight. One minute I was the assistant manager of a Premiership club and then suddenly I was out of work wondering where the next job would come from.

The answer to that question came a few weeks later with a call from *Sky* football commentator, Alan Parry, someone I had known for many years and who had become a very good friend during that time. As well as his television work, Alan was also passionate about his local football team, Wycombe Wanderers, and some years earlier had become a director of the club. He phoned me one day when I was over at my daughter's to say that Wycombe manager Lawrie Sanchez was leaving and asked whether I'd be interested in taking over in a caretaker capacity. Lawrie had done great things at the club, including getting them to the FA Cup semi-finals, but at the time of Alan's phone call the side were near the bottom of League Two. The next day I went along to have a meeting with Wycombe chairman, Ivor Beeks, and it was agreed that I'd take over at the club and see what I could do while they gave themselves time to look for a new manager.

Things went well and although we only got one win during the month I was caretaker, we played some good football and notched up a couple of important draws. There was a decent spirit and I think the players responded well to what I was trying to do. Wycombe held interviews for the vacant manager's job and said that if I wanted to be considered I would have to go through the same process as everyone else who had applied, which was only fair. On the day I went for my interview Glenn called me to say that there might be something happening with regard to him getting another job, and that it might be a foreign club. I went into the Wycombe interview feeling quite relaxed, because I suppose that at the back of my mind I was thinking I might be going with Glenn again if he got a new job. During the course of the interview I was actually asked what I would do if Glenn got a big job and asked me to be his assistant once more. I joked that if it was Barcelona I suppose I'd have to go! But I later found out that the doubt about me leaving weighed against me when it came to making a decision. In the end the club decided to give the job to Tony Adams, his first in management, and they also asked me whether I would be his assistant, which I agreed to do.

Tony's first game in charge came three days after he was officially unveiled as the new Wycombe boss at a press conference. It was a home FA Cup first round tie against one of my old clubs, Swindon. He was happy for me to take the team while he watched and we put in a really good performance to win the game 4-1. Our next match was at home in the league against Brentford and Tony decided that when it came to defending set plays the team would use zonal, rather than the man-to-man marking I'd had them using during my time in charge. We lost the game 2-1 conceding the goals from set-pieces, and I quickly realised that I didn't think things would work out. I said as much to Tony, not just because of the way he'd asked the team to mark, but because I felt he was a young manager with his own ideas, and maybe I just wasn't the right person for him to have as an assistant. Perhaps I was a bit hasty, but once I'd made my mind up that was it. Tony was fantastic about it all and I think he understood the situation and how I felt.

My stay at Wycombe Wanderers had been short and sweet. This time I had made the decision myself and not been sacked, but I was still out of work – again!

CHAPTER 15

RETURN TO THE WANDERERS

I suppose I'd been quite lucky since coming back to England from the States all those years earlier, because I hadn't ever really been out of work for long periods of time, despite all the moves I'd made, but things certainly changed for me after my decision to leave Wycombe.

It seemed fine to begin with and I enjoyed being able to spend time with Myra and get on with things like painting my house and doing my art work. I probably thought that something would come along fairly quickly, but as the year came to an end there was still no sign that anything was going to happen. By the time spring came around I was getting a bit concerned, because although I'd earned good money during my time at Tottenham, I was in no position to be able to sit back and not worry about my finances.

GORY TALES

I've already said that Myra had always worried about me not working, and although she never said anything, I knew that like me she was growing concerned at the lack of job offers.

Whether I was in work or not I wanted to make sure I kept up to date with all my coaching and went off and completed my Pro Licence. By that time I had been out of full-time work for months, although I had at least been able to stay in touch with the game by doing some scouting for the FA. It was good to be watching decent games and Premiership players, but I still knew I needed a job.

An unlikely chance did come along when I was contacted by Conference side Forest Green Rovers. They asked if I'd be interested in becoming manager and whether I would go for an interview. It was just going to be a short-term thing and I was happy with that, because at least it meant I would be working with players again. But at the interview I was a bit surprised when they asked me what experience I'd had at that level. I had to say none. I'd just come from coaching Tottenham Hotspur!

I was also in the frame when Hibs began looking for a new manager. I had never really considered going back to manage in Scotland, but the more I thought about it the more both Myra and I liked the idea. I went for two interviews with them and thought I could have done a good job up there. When it came to talking about my personal terms I asked them for a similar salary to the one I'd been earning at Tottenham, and I don't think they were really prepared to pay me the sort of money I thought was fair for the job. In the end they plumped for Tony Mowbray, who I knew from my brief spell with Ipswich, and he went on to do a fantastic job for them before moving on to WBA in more recent years, where he had success in getting them into the Premier League.

John Gorman

The summer came and went without any definite offer but as autumn approached the phone rang one day and it was Gillingham chairman Paul Scally. Andy Hessenthaler had done a tremendous job for the Gills since being appointed player-manager four years earlier, and had got them punching above their weight with some fantastic performances in the Championship. For a club of Gillingham's size and resources to be playing in a league like that was a marvellous achievement, and Andy had done brilliantly to keep them playing at that level. Paul explained that the team were going through a sticky patch and asked whether I'd be interested in coming in to give Andy a hand and take some of the burden off him. Andy knew about the whole idea and was fine about it all. It was a very loose arrangement and I went in and tried to help brighten things up a bit. I got on well with Andy and although the results weren't fantastic, the spirit and enthusiasm of the players was really good.

From my point of view it was nice to be back working with players on a daily basis and at a club I still had a lot of affection for. After all, Gillingham had given me my break in coaching and I had some fond memories from my time with them back in the 1980's, but I never really saw the job as being permanent.

Towards the end of November Gillingham played away at Crewe in a league game and lost 4-1. It was a result that left us one off the bottom in the Championship. It meant that the following week's game against Nottingham Forest was going to be huge because they were also having a bad time near the foot of the table, so both sides desperately needed the points. A couple of weeks earlier Tony Adams had left Wycombe a little more than a year after he had been appointed manager. It meant the club were looking for a new manager and I got a call from my old mate Alan Parry once again asking if I would be interested in coming back. It wasn't something I had to think twice about. I'd enjoyed being at Wycombe and the chance of going back as the manager really appealed to me. They wanted me to go for an interview, which happened to be arranged for the Tuesday after the Crewe game.

Then on the morning of the interview it was decided that Andy would step down as Gillingham manager, and they wanted me to take temporary charge of the team. So there I was going off for an interview to become the Wycombe manager, knowing that the next day I would be taking charge of the Gillingham team as they prepared for one of the biggest games of their season so far.

As soon as news got out about Andy there was the inevitable speculation about me taking over from him on a permanent basis as the new manager, but I knew I'd had a good interview at Wycombe and felt pretty confident about getting the job there. I took charge of the team for the Forest game and we managed to get a great win beating them 2-1. Lots of the questions in the press conference afterwards were about whether I thought winning the game had given me a good chance of getting the Gillingham job, and also about whether I was going to apply for it. I told everyone that I was just pleased we had won and tried to leave it at that, knowing that the Wycombe job was a strong possibility for me. Sure enough Wycombe did offer me the job and the chance to return to the Wanderers, which I happily took. So I left Gillingham having been in charge for just one game – and with a 100 per cent record!

I was delighted to be going back to Wycombe. The place felt right for me and I knew I could do a good job for them. I was excited at the prospect of being a manager again and I could tell that Myra was happy and contented with the prospect of me working for them. For almost four months neither of us really had a care in the world, and I loved the job from the very first day. The team began to play some very decent stuff and I knew that the play-offs were a real possibility for the club after the disappointment of relegation the previous season. Things couldn't really have been better.

As I said at the beginning of this book, life seemed good as I prepared the team for that trip to Cambridge back in mid-March 2005, but then life can sometimes kick you in the teeth.

CHAPTER 16

THE LOVE OF MY LIFE

When the full impact of what had happened finally hit me I was left with an enormous emptiness in my life. As I said at the start of my story, Myra's death and her funeral was a strange experience for me and it really did feel as if it was happening to someone else. I think it was because I couldn't quite take in what had happened and I tried to make sure I kept myself busy and did normal things.

Two days after the funeral Wycombe were due to play an away league game at Cheltenham. We were second in the table and they were seventh. It was a big game for both clubs. As ridiculous as it may seem I actually went to the match, I shouldn't have really, but I thought it was the right thing to do

John Gorman

at the time. It got me back to work with something to concentrate on and with the team riding high in the league I felt a responsibility to be there. We were 1-0 up, they got a penalty and we ended up losing 2-1, as well as having one of our players, Kevin Betsy, sent off. After the game I steamed into the referee's room and absolutely slaughtered the official. I went mad and they even had to get a steward in to come and get me. It was crazy and I should never have done it. I suppose I was still very drained and emotional after all that had gone on that week and the FA actually wrote to me saying that because of the circumstances they weren't going to take further action.

We managed to win our next game which was at home against Shrewsbury and our fans gave me a marvellous reception, but despite playing well in matches after that we just couldn't win. To be more precise, we kept on losing. Six on the bounce and we went from being second in the league and looking like automatic promotion candidates, to sixth place in the table. One of the games we lost was against Torquay who were struggling near the foot of the league. At the end of the game Ivor Beeks happened to ask how on earth we could lose 1-0 to Torquay. I swore at him. I was even getting angry with the chairman.

After we'd lost our sixth game in a row I went to the board and said that maybe it would be better if I had a break and let my coaches, Steve Brown and Keith Ryan take over, which was what they did. Their first game in charge was away at bottom club Rushden & Diamonds and Wycombe won 3-1, meanwhile I flew to America for a break with friends in Tampa. A lot of people we'd both known over there had heard what had happened to Myra, and while I was in Tampa some of the ex-Rowdie lads who I had played with, organised a tribute to her. About 75 people turned up, including Perry Van der Beck, Peter Anderson, Neil Roberts, Wes McLeod, and Rodney Marsh who happened to be in Florida at the time. It was a lovely thing to do, and soon after the funeral we'd had another tribute to Myra back in Edinburgh, because a lot of people from Scotland had been unable to make it down.

Going to Tampa did me a lot of good and when I phoned home and spoke to Nick and Amanda I told both of them I felt a lot better and that the break had really helped me. I felt refreshed. I was still the Wycombe manager and by this time the team were in the play-offs and due to meet Cheltenham in a semi-final over two legs. When I got back Steve Hayes phoned and basically said that although everyone at the club thought the world of me, they felt that I wasn't quite right to come back and take over running the team again. I have to say I was disappointed and at the time I thought they were wrong, but if I look at it from their point of view I can see where they were coming from.

They knew how much Myra's death had affected me, and probably felt they were doing me a favour by taking away the pressure and stress of having a team taking part in the play-offs. I ended up going to Scotland for a few days and watched the first leg against Cheltenham on television. Wycombe were at home for that game and lost 2-1, with the second match ending in a goalless draw. It meant that after all the hard work, good play and good performances the team had put in during the course of the season, they missed out on promotion and I was bitterly disappointed for them. They were a great bunch of lads who had worked so hard for me. They had suffered the emotional turmoil of losing poor Mark Philo, and then seen their manager lose his wife. It had been tough for them and to come so close before missing out must have been a horrible experience.

With the season over for Wycombe Steve asked me if I could pop into the club for a meeting just over a week after the team had lost out to Cheltenham. Everyone at the club seemed pleased to see me, there were hugs all round and I chatted to my personal assistant Deborah about returning, but when I went in for the meeting it became clear Steve and Ivor felt it was best if I parted company with the club. A statement was put together saying as much and I was out of work again. Steve in particular was adamant that it was the right thing for me, because of my health and what had happened, even though I told him that I felt fine and wanted to get back to my job. Steve was only trying to do what he thought best for me and nobody could have been kinder or more helpful than he was when Myra was undergoing all of her treatment and I had to make regular visits to the hospital. He had to make his decision, but it was a sad end to my time at a lovely club and I wish things could have worked out differently.

I wasn't the only one about to leave a football club, because four days later my mate Colin Calderwood left Northampton, having led them to promotion from League Two, and had been installed as the new boss at Nottingham Forest. Colin had put my name forward to the Northampton chairman, David Cardoza as a possible replacement for him. By this time I had already had two interviews, one for the director of football job at Lincoln and the other for manager of Hartlepool. I was determined to get back into work quickly, and when Northampton phoned to ask if I could go and talk to them about their managerial vacancy less than a week after leaving Wycombe, I was happy to say yes. Within 24 hours they had called back and said that they wanted me to take over from Colin. I was a manager again, in double-quick time.

The Northampton chairman had apparently always liked the way my teams played football and I promised him and the supporters that I was going to try and do the same for them. We had a good pre-season and began the league campaign with a draw at Crewe, before losing home games against Brentford and Forest and then winning at Gillingham. Those matches seemed to set a pattern for what was to come. We were great away, but just couldn't win our home games. We had one defeat in 11 league games on our travels and only one win in 11 home games. The last of those 11 home games came against Leyton Orient in December, who beat us 1-0 after we'd played really well. Orient were managed by my friend Martin Ling, who had been one of my players at Swindon.

"I'm going to quit," I told him when he came into my office for a chat after the game.

"Don't be stupid John," he said. "You played really well and the home results will start to come."

But my decision had nothing to do with the results at our Sixfields Stadium, it was all to do with the way I felt about my life. Northampton were a great little club and the chairman was really supportive. Not doing well at home was frustrating, but like Martin had said that would change at some stage. I just didn't have the desire I'd had before. I didn't want to carry on doing the job.

I had a meeting with the chairman the next day and told him I wanted to leave. He was disappointed and tried to persuade me to stay, but my mind was made up. A statement was put out saying that I had resigned for personal reasons, and when I was interviewed I said that I couldn't be bothered with all the pressure of trying to win football games at that time.

I probably used the wrong word when I mentioned "pressure." It wasn't pressure, because I'd been used to dealing with that right through my career, it was more a case of my whole working life feeling a bit meaningless without Myra. We had been together for so long and she knew me inside out. She was there through the good and bad times and knew exactly what I was thinking without me having to say a word. This may sound strange but she was at her best when things weren't going well for me in football. If we'd just lost a game or the team were having a bad run, she had an uncanny knack of being able to say the right thing and put it all into perspective. When I was at Northampton if we lost a game at home or hadn't managed to get the result we deserved I'd come home and there was nobody in the house. Of course I had family and friends to talk to. They were always there for me and always supportive. I saw a lot of Amanda, Rick, Nick and Jay, as well as my little grandkids, Aaron and Josie. They were all wonderful and a joy to be with. I also had people like Les O'Neill, whose own wife Anne had died from breast cancer four months after Myra. He was fantastic and has continued to give me great support. Glenn and his wife Vee, Richard and Paula, Barbs, who was Myra's hairdresser and a great help and Yopi who was another good friend to Myra, Jim Barron and Mal, as well as Tommy Cannon, were great and I could pick up the phone day or night and speak to them. But there was no Myra, just a gap in my life. It didn't matter how much I tried to fill that gap by making sure I was working and always busy.

The truth was I had lost the love of my life.

CHAPTER 17

STARTING AGAIN

After I had made the decision to leave Northampton I felt relieved. It gave me time to think about my life and decide what I was going to do next. For once I was in no hurry to rush back into work.

I'd left the job five days before Christmas and the holiday period wasn't easy for me or the kids. It was our first without Myra and we all desperately missed her, but at the same time we were able to remember all the great years we'd had together as a family and we'd shared some wonderful times. It must be the same for anyone who has lost a loved one. Things like Christmas, an anniversary, or a birthday always bring back memories. They are never easy times.

One of the first things I did early in 2007 was decide to put my house in Binfield on the market. It was too big for just me and there were a lot of

John Gorman

memories every time I walked into the place. It had been our dream home and we'd had great times there, but I just felt it was right to sell it and move to something smaller which is exactly what I did. The house went in March and on the day I sold it I moved to a two bedroom apartment not very far away. I still loved the area and Myra had been buried nearby. I had a lot of friends there so it made sense to stay around in a place that had become so familiar. I also had to give our dog to Myra's sister Eileen. I had bought it for Myra and she'd called it Raasey, after an Island in Scotland. It had become a big part of both our lives and it was a wrench when he had to go, but at least he went to Eileen and having been up to see him since, I know he's settled in really well. Perhaps he has some Scottish blood in him!

Although I hadn't rushed back to work, I did agree to do some scouting for the FA, which I really enjoyed and towards the end of the football season they had arranged for me to go to Holland and watch the Euro under-21 Championships. I was looking forward to the trip and was beginning to feel much better about my life. Time does help to heal, and even though I knew I would always miss Myra and that things could never be the same without her, I also realised that I had to try to move on with my own life. Not having a full-time job probably helped at the time, because I was able to do things without having the same sort of day-to-day responsibilities I would have had if I'd been working for a club. I also did a bit of travelling, visiting the property I'd bought in Spain, a house Myra was never able to see because she had been too unwell to travel when the villa had been built.

While I was in Spain I got a call from George Burley who had done really well since taking over at Southampton as their manager and the side were heading towards the play-offs. He and his wife Jill had been good friends to me and he asked if I fancied going to watch a game at St Mary's. When I got back from Spain I went to watch the first leg of their play-off semi-final at home against Derby, which they lost 2-1. They won the second leg 3-2, evening the scores up but then missed out 4-3 on penalties, ending their hopes of playing in the Premier League. George had a chat with me and asked whether I would consider working for him as the club's chief scout. It was the sort of role I had never considered in the past, but it seemed to be the right job at the right time. I had an interview at the club and was offered the post, teaming up with George for a second time. Ironically, he'd phoned me up when he was manager of Derby and asked if I fancied working with him, but at that time I had just said yes to Paul Scally about working alongside Andy Hessenthaler at Gillingham and I couldn't go back on my word.

I'd had some time off and felt much better for it so when the new season began in the summer of 2007, I felt really refreshed and was looking forward to getting stuck into my new job. George also let me take some of the training during the pre-season period, and I found myself really enjoying the experience. The trouble was, I hadn't been employed as a coach and being a full-time chief scout was a whole new world to me. I got on with the job, but if I'm honest I don't think I did it as well as I would have liked, simply because I didn't have as good a knowledge of players from all the leagues as I would have liked. That only comes from being in the job for a while and I was new to it all, but I loved being back at Southampton and George is a good manager who I enjoyed working for. He let me get involved with the first team, because as well as looking at players, I would also look at the opposition and give my input when it came to analysing other teams and how Southampton should maybe approach a game. Results didn't go as well as everyone had hoped after getting to the play-offs in the previous season, and there was probably a lot of expectation because Southampton is a big club with strong support and the stadium at St Mary's is superb.

After just failing to take Scotland to the Euro '08 finals, Alex McLeish had moved back into club management with Birmingham City, prompting a search for a new national manager and at the end of January 2008 the Scottish FA announced they had found their man. George Burley. It was no real surprise to me, because George had all the qualities they must have been looking for and I think the job came along at just the right time for him. While it was great for George, it was obviously a problem for Southampton but they decided to solve it in the short-term by putting me in charge with Jason Dodd, who had been a player for the Saints and had come back as a coach.

It didn't take me long to get the old buzz back as soon as I stepped onto the training pitch. Although Jason and I were officially in joint charge, I was the more senior of the partnership and I was determined the team were going to go out and enjoy their football. We both wanted the side to be attractive to watch, but we also wanted them to get the results the club needed. Despite some bad results the board must have liked what we were trying to do, because they called us in one day and said that we had the job until the end of the season. We put in some great performances but didn't get the reward the lads deserved. In one game at Stoke we found ourselves three down in the first half and I really laid into them at the break. After half-time we were a different team and scored two goals but could have ended up with five and were really unlucky not to come away with something against a team who eventually got promoted to the Premier League.

Soon after that game we faced a tricky match at League Two side Bristol Rovers in an FA Cup fifth round tie. Rovers were two divisions below us but had home advantage, a fanatical support and a pitch that looked as though it was made for a cup upset. It was a lunchtime kick-off and live on TV. I got terrible stick in the dug-out from the first whistle because of my time at Bristol City, and we were never able to get to grips with the game. It stayed goalless in the first half but there was no denying Rovers were enjoying things more than us and were the better team. They were ready to scrap and fight for everything in true underdog fashion, and we found it hard to cope with them.

It looked as though we might get away with a draw and take them back to St Mary's, but with six minutes remaining Rickie Lambert scored for Rovers and we never looked capable of getting back into the game. The TV people had got what they wanted, Southampton were on the wrong end of an FA Cup upset, and our chance of a quarter-final place had disappeared. After the game I spoke to the board and just said that they should do what they felt they had to do. Two days later Nigel Pearson was appointed as the new Southampton manager. That's football as they say.

It was a shame things had worked out as they had against Rovers, but the club obviously felt they needed to make a change. The FA Cup disappointment was one thing, but results in the league had not gone well and they didn't want the club slipping into League One. I had no problem with Nigel coming in and as far as I was concerned I wanted to help in any way I could. For the first few games I found myself involved, but then things started to change and towards the end of the season it was pretty clear he didn't want me around the first team. Sometimes things like that happen. We just didn't seem to hit it off. Southampton managed to preserve their Championship status although it went right down to the wire. I fully expected to be sacked by the club, because I couldn't see Nigel wanting me around for the new season. I did eventually leave after Rupert Lowe, who had left the club, returned as a major player in May. But I wasn't the only one to go from St Mary's, because so did Nigel, when Southampton decided to go Dutch and appointed Jan Poortvliet as their new manager.

To be honest I had already resigned myself to leaving and had been talking to Glenn about a project he had been working on for some time. After George left there was a lot of talk about Glenn coming back as Southampton manager, and the fans seemed very keen on the idea, but I knew that was never likely to happen. Not because he didn't like the club, it was simply a case of him being too involved in setting up the Glenn Hoddle Academy in Spain. He'd put a lot of his own time, money and effort into getting the scheme going and in the process had turned down several job offers. I knew he was really serious about it and after the season ended he asked whether I would be interested in joining him to help coach at the Academy. I'd told Southampton from the first day I sat down with George that there could be a time when Glenn wanted me to work with him again. I was quite up front about it and everyone at the club knew.

The idea of the Academy is for it to offer a route back into professional football for some of the young players who are discarded by the system. Every year right across Europe clubs release loads of talented youngsters, and Glenn has felt for some time that decisions on their futures are made too soon. If they are given maybe another year or two to develop then they could make it as full-time professional players. During the summer of 2008 Glenn's dream became a reality and I loved the idea of teaming up with him again to do what I feel I do best – coach.

I am now heavily involved in working with him on the project. He has put together a great little team to help him run things, including my fellow coaches Graham Rix and Nigel Spackman. I love coaching the youngsters and once again I enjoy working one-on-one with the players, trying to help improve their individual game and give them a way back into professional football. I certainly have my appetite back and just love being out on the training pitch. It has been good for me.

Football has been such a big part of my life and it's great to be involved in something as new and exciting as this. The game has a way of lifting your spirits and I get the same thrill out of kicking a ball now as I did when I was a wee lad back in Scotland trying to juggle a football and hold those pots and pans that my granny had given me.

Quite recently I had a few days break in the South of France, and purely by chance met Jean Tigana, the brilliant former French international and Fulham manager. We didn't really know each other but got chatting and he asked me back to his magnificent home and vineyard. Jean kept saying that he was so lucky because the ability to play football had given him such a fabulous lifestyle. We ended up playing "keepie-uppie" in his garden, like a couple of kids, and it made me realise just how lucky I was as well to have earned my living from a game. If I hadn't made it as a professional player, I would still have kicked a ball about with my mates and played in parks teams. So would Tigana and so would any of the top professional players in the Premier League. They might be earning a fortune compared to the money I was on at places like Carlisle, when we trained in kit that was often falling apart, but the love of the game remains the same. I'm not bitter about the money on offer to modern players. Times change, it's a different era and we all have to move on.

On a personal note, I'm now seeing a really nice lady called Denise who is very understanding about my feelings for Myra. She's been good for me. So have Nick and Amanda. Nick is now in Thailand with Jay, and I feel lucky to have a great son who is also a fantastic friend as well. Jay has been really good for him and she was also marvellous when Myra was ill during the last weeks of her life. I know the two of them became very close. Amanda and Rick have been magnificent and I know just how difficult she has found it to cope with the loss of her mother. She is a dream daughter and a wonderful mother. I know Myra would be proud of her and of our two wonderful grandchildren, Aaron, and Josie, who continue to bring real joy into my life.

Myra suffered dreadfully near the end of her life, but there is a comfort in knowing that she is at peace now. She is buried in a very beautiful spot surrounded by the sort of countryside she loved so much. I'd actually had a conversation with her just before she died about where her grave should be and we decided it would be near our home instead of in Scotland, because we would be able to visit more easily. After she was laid to rest I walked out of the graveyard and couldn't help smiling to myself. Directly opposite was the village football field, she'd put up with me and the game for all those years and there was still no escape!

God bless you darling.